SocialSquad

EMPOWERED WITH KNOWLEDGE

A Curriculum for Creating a Social Skill Group
Including Peers as Models and Advocates

By Nicole Bain, PhD & Kathie Davis

socialsquads@gmail.com

Social Squad—Empowered with Knowledge

A Curriculum for Creating a Social Skill Group Including Peers as Models and Advocates

Illustrations by Kathie Davis

Printed by CreateSpace, An Amazon.com Company

socialsquads@gmail.com

Contents

Introduction

What are Social Squads and what does it take to set one up in your school?

Social Squads were developed to provide an opportunity for typically developing children (Peer Mentors) to mentor their peer who has challenges with social skills (child of focus). These groups were designed with the following principles in mind:

- Children learn best from their peers.
- Educating peers with facts eliminates the need for students to guess why certain peers behave differently than most others and helps to foster empathy and compassion rather than confusion, frustration, and even sometimes fear.
- Providing information and practice for best ways to support each other reduces bullying and isolation.
- Mentors make great advocates in the classroom, playground and other school and community settings.

Therefore, Social Squads are made up of a mixed group of students bringing typically developing peers alongside children with social challenges. The child of focus might be a student with Autism, ADHD or perhaps a student with social challenges due to other life factors.

Selecting Squad Members

Squad members should be hand selected. It's best to make the groups even numbered as there are several partner activities. Four is a good total number of students in a Squad, so that means you'll be looking for three peers that have some of these attributes: respectful attitude, natural leader, compassionate or empathetic (or capable of becoming that way), ability to maintain confidentiality (this is played up with the students and we have not had any breaches of confidentiality), and good role models. Not all Squad members will have all of these attributes. Some Squads may include students who may not be considered the child of focus but may exhibit one or two social challenges and need to be learning skills covered in the sessions.

Selecting an Adult Squad Leader

Squads need to be led by a staff member that will have at least some contact with the child of focus throughout the school day beyond the weekly Squad meetings. This adult can be the school counselor, behavior specialist, para educator, special education teacher, or classroom teacher. Their time commitment will involve approximately one hour per week for the group (30 minutes for prep and 30 minutes for actual group meeting time) as well as at least a few minutes per day to check in with the child of focus and/or the peer mentors to make sure everyone is growing and learning to use the skills presented during the meetings.

Topics Covered During Squad Meetings

Topics covered during Social Squad meetings are varied depending on the specific needs of the child of focus and the dynamics of the group. In general we cover the following issues:

- All people have strengths and challenges; we encourage ways to support each other given what they learn about the strengths and challenges of their friends in the group.
- How to have a brief "chat" with others.
- Thought vs. Talk using thought and talk bubbles along with a brain filter to know when to think it and when to say it.
- Perspective taking and understanding that others have different thoughts than you.

- Who the people in your universe are (friends, family, acquaintances and strangers) and when/where/what you can say to the different people in those different categories.
- Sensory differences.
- Positive and negative actions and words.
- BIG DEAL and little deal; distinguishing the difference and how to respond appropriately to each.
- Emotions and emotion regulation.

You can add to or alter any of the lessons to fit the specific situation with the students involved. In fact, it is not our intent that this manual should be used cover to cover in its entirety. We envision our materials to be used as a guide for helping lead Social Squads that will address the specific needs of the many students that can benefit from adult facilitated interactions with typical peers. While we recommend that you follow the format of the first three lessons fairly closely, it's after that point that you will begin to choose the order of when and how you want to present the remaining lessons. As you can see, we've included activities for 14 lessons, while groups are only expected to last for 8-10 weeks.

We do strongly recommend that each meeting begin with a "chat practice" as repetition is essential for students with social challenges to learn appropriate conversation skills. Over time, you may expand the chat format to teach more advanced conversation skills to the child of focus, reminding that child of the importance of "back and forth" conversations versus dominating a conversation. This will involve specific teaching of how and why to show an interest in other's hobbies and activities. Having peers involved in the lessons also allows you the opportunity to help them understand how to proactively redirect the child of focus outside of weekly meetings.

Duration and Location of Squad Meetings

Groups are designed to meet for one-half hour per week and to last from 8 to 10 weeks depending on the number of lessons the team feels they need to address and the overall success of the Squad as they move forward. You can include a couple of sessions during the 8-10 weeks where the child of focus is not present so that the others can share openly about their concerns and be given some appropriate tips on coping with and supporting the child of focus. Outside of the weekly meetings, we offer "weekly challenges" to the members that include ways to interact more frequently in a positive way with each other throughout the school day.

Meetings need to be held in a location that is private enough for all members to feel confident about sharing without fear of non-Squad members listening or judging. Meetings can be held in small conference rooms or in classrooms. If it is decided that meetings will be held during lunchtime, make sure you have an alternative location to the open lunchroom.

How to Use Squad Lessons

Each lesson is designed to help you easily prepare for and conduct sessions as well as follow up with parents on what their child learned each week. The layout is as follows:

- Materials for this week's group—a complete list of all materials needed, including a list of what worksheets need to be printed from the manual.
- Review (except for Lesson 1 and Lesson 2)—a brief script of how to open each week's session.
- Discussion—introduces the concept of the week.
- Activity—describes the activity used to reinforce the discussion of this week's concept.

- Mission of the Week—an important section to remember each week as it is here that the reminder goes out to all members to stay connected and supportive of each other outside of group time.
- Squad Report—to be printed and sent (or emailed) home with the child of focus in the group to help their parents to be kept informed of the concepts being learned. It is also an encouragement to parents to practice and support these skills.

The "Sample Letter/Permission Form" should be sent home to the parent/guardian of the child of focus along with the "Beginning Survey" (2 pages) and "What is a Social Squad" for parent/guardian to have all information regarding a Social Squad and how it will benefit their child.

Sample Letter/Permission Form for Parent/Guardian of Child of Focus

Dear_____,

Your child has been identified as a student who may benefit from taking part in a Social Squad. A Social Squad consists of your child (the mentee) and their peers (the mentors) who have been identified as good social role models. Students in the Social Squad will learn more about your child and are encouraged to get to know him/her better through daily conversations and time spent together at our weekly Squad Meetings. An important concept that is taught and followed up throughout the lessons will be confidentiality. All Squad Members are expected to be confidential about the discussions conducted during the weekly meetings. The peers in your child's Squad are also taught to give social feedback to your child when needed. We have meetings for the purpose of socializing, getting to know each other better, and most importantly, to teach your child social skills alongside peers in a structured setting. The purpose of this Social Squad is to promote feelings of belonging in the school community.

If you have any questions, feel free to call or e-mail me at:_____

Please sign below if you give permission for your child to be part of a Social Squad.

Sincerely,

....

I give Permission for my child to participate in a Social Squad at school.

__ Yes, my child's disability information can be shared with the Squad members on an as needed basis.

__ No, I do not want my child's disability information shared with their Squad members.

_____

(Parent Signature)   (Date)

Social Squad Parent/Guardian/Teacher Beginning Survey

Member Name:_____ Date:_____

Filled in by:_____

My child's strengths are:_____

_____

My child's favorite interests are:_____

_____

I have these concerns about my child:_____

_____

These are things that I find to be triggers for my child:_____

_____

I would like to see these social skills improve:_____

_____

My child's friends at home are:_____

_____.

My child's friends at school are:_____

_____

Anything else you'd like us to know about your child:_____

_____

_____

_____

_____

_____

_____

Directions: Based on your observations in various situations, rate the child's use of the following skills according to the scale:

1 = child **almost never** uses the skill   4 = child **often** uses the skill
2 = child **seldom** uses the skill   5 = child **almost always** uses the skill
3 = child **sometimes** uses the skill

1) Socially appropriate listening posture _____
   Comment:_____

2) Maintaining a conversation _____
   Comment:_____

3) Starting a conversation _____
   Comment:_____

4) Joining a conversation _____
   Comment:_____

5) Sensitive topics _____
   Comment:_____

6) Playing a game _____
   Comment:_____

7) Asking others to play _____
   Comment:_____

8) Compromising _____
   Comment:_____

9) Keeping calm _____
   Comment:_____

10) Dealing with mistakes _____
    Comment:_____

11) Understanding others' feelings _____
    Comment:_____

12) Dealing with teasing _____
    Comment:_____

13) Maintaining personal space _____
    Comment:_____

WHAT IS A SOCIAL SQUAD?

Social Squads are being developed to better support students in elementary schools who may have challenges in the social arena. Some students struggle to make good social connections with their peers. These groups are formed specifically to meet the needs of these students by providing them with an opportunity to work in a small group with good social models (Peer Mentors). The concept of a Social Squad was designed with the following principles in mind:

- Children learn social skills best from their peers.
- Educating peers with facts eliminates the need for students to guess why certain peers behave differently than most others and helps to foster empathy and compassion rather than confusion, frustration and even sometimes fear.
- Providing information and practice for best ways to support each other reduces bullying and isolation.
- Mentors make great advocates in the classroom, playground and other school and community settings.

The following are commonly asked questions and answers regarding these dynamic new groups.

Q: Who is in a Social Squad?
A: One or two students that are identified as needing help with social skills, especially with their peers. Also included are between two and four peers who have good social skills and exhibit leadership qualities.

Q: Are these formal groups and who leads them?
A: Yes. Each group of children is specially selected by staff in our school, and weekly Squad meetings are led by one or two staff members.

Q: Are these groups only for students with Autism?
A: Definitely not. While several of the students we create these groups for do have Autism, other students may struggle to make social connections for a variety of reasons. Sometimes students are new to this country and may be a bit shy or uncertain about social customs. Some students just find social situations difficult.

Q: Will my child miss instructional time in his/her class?
A: Possibly. Each group is individually structured to meet the needs of the student identified as needing additional social skills support. Meetings are held one time per week, and every effort is made to find a time best suited for the student and their peers to not miss out on critical instructional time. Often this is resolved by having the meetings during lunch and/or recess time. Older elementary students that don't participate in band or music may have group meetings during band/orchestra time when teachers are not providing whole group instruction.

Q: How long are the meetings and do they last all year?
A: Meetings are scheduled for thirty minutes. The groups are not intended to last for an entire school year although there is no defined number of weeks. A minimum of six weeks is recommended and generally lasting until the end of the grading period.

Q: What if I allow my child to participate and then change my mind?
A: As your child's parent or guardian you always have the right to alter plans developed for your child. However, you are encouraged to have a discussion with the Social Squad adult leader and/or your child's IEP manager about your concerns before making a decision to end a group.

Q: What will you tell the other students about my child?

A: Based on your responses indicated on the parent permission form, we will share information about your child that will help his/her peers understand why they may have certain behaviors or responses to them in social settings. The peers will be taught good ways of modeling appropriate social interactions for your child as well as help to advocate for them in the greater school setting.

Q: Will I know what they are working on in the groups each week?

A: Please check in with your child to see if they are able to share information on what happened at group each week. We will send home weekly Squad Reports which may include worksheets with information on how they were used in group and how you might follow through with the lessons or common language at home. For instance, we will talk about such things as: I Think/You Think (understanding other people have different perspectives); Positive and Negative Behavior; Thought Bubbles vs. Talk Bubbles (and using your brain to filter when to say or not say things); Who are the People in Your Personal Universe (identifying family, friends, acquaintances and strangers); and Talking Tips for things you should or should not say to different people.

Sample Letter/Permission Form for Parents of Peer Mentors

Dear_____,

Your child has been identified as a good social role model and chosen to participate in a Social Squad to help their peers build social skills.

A Social Squad is a group of peers who agree to interact with a student, the mentee, who has challenges learning social skills. Being in a Social Squad involves your son/daughter having daily conversations, periodically having lunch together, providing social skills feedback to the mentee, communicating with the Social Squad facilitator, and meeting once a week with the group members to learn new social skills alongside the peer they are supporting while also sharing progress and brainstorming ideas on how to help their peer develop his/her social skills. A Social Squad is beneficial for both the mentee and the mentor. The mentee has the opportunity to interact with peers on a daily basis, practicing social skills while feeling accepted at school. At the same time, your child (the mentor) is able to be a good role model and learn about accepting individuals with differences. We also stress the importance of confidentiality for all discussions that occur during the weekly meetings.

This is a completely voluntary endeavor; feel free to discuss this with your child and call or email me at - _____ if you have any questions. Please sign and return this form if you give permission for your child to participate in a Social Squad.

Thank you!

Sincerely,

....

I give Permission for my child to participate in a Social Squad.

_____

(Parent Signature)   (Date)

SocialSquad

Sample Letter to Alert Staff in the Building to the Formation and Purpose of a Squad

We want to make you aware of an exciting new program that a few of our students are embarking upon. The program is called Social Squad. Social Squad is an intervention designed to support students with Autism or social/communication deficits to help them connect with peers in a more appropriate way. The Social Squad is a group of typically developing students (in this instance, __add peer names here__) and a student with a disability (in this instance, _add child of focus's name_____.) The students meet weekly with 1-2 adults (__can add in adult names and titles here_) who will help them learn skills to support and include a peer with disabilities. The Social Squad members are being asked to help others who might have difficulty communicating and/or who might need help fitting in, and they will be learning how to give gentle reminders to _(child of focus)_____. The benefit of the program is that all students will learn some new social skills and other peers may begin to catch on and extend pro-social behaviors.

We want you to be aware of this program so that if you find one of these students providing suggestions to ___(child of focus)_____, you'll be aware of the reason why. These students are eager to help and might be trying to figure out how best to interact and share these suggestions. If you find that the Social Squad members are giving suggestions at inopportune times, please gently let the Squad member know when would be a better time to do this.

Thank you for your support. This is an exciting opportunity to build advocacy skills in our students. If you have any further questions about the Social Squad or activities involving these students, you may contact

_____.

Lesson 1: Mentors Only

Lesson 1: Mentors Only

Materials for this week's group

- Enough copies of the Social Squad Surveys for each member to complete
  NOTE: There are two different surveys for two different ability levels
    - Worksheet #1 (pages 1 & 2) is designed for nonreaders/grades 1 & 2
    - Worksheet #2 is designed for upper elementary or secondary
- Pens or pencils for all

Welcome

Sample dialogue: "You are now a Social Squad member. You were selected due to your good leadership and friendship skills."

Discussion

Discuss confidentiality (e.g., what does it mean, who you can and can't share the group discussions with, etc.).

Sample dialogue: "You will have a chance to learn more about the members of this group and their strengths and challenges. This is information that stays in this group, so what is said in group stays in group."

Next introduce the purpose of the group.

Sample dialogue: "The purpose of this group is to support a student(s) in your class that has a difficult time making friends and 'fitting in' with their peers at school. The student(s) you are supporting is (insert receiving student's name here. For this passage we will use the name *Joey*). "

Ask members to discuss what strengths they have seen the receiving student exhibit.

Sample dialogue: "What have you seen that Joey is really good at?" If they need some ideas, share what you know, such as "I know Joey is really good at geography," or "Did you know Joey loves cars? He can tell you the names of over one hundred different types of cars."

"What other things have you noticed about Joey in class?"

If the mentors are stumped, you can probe: "Does Joey seem to get along with others? Does he have a lot of friends in class? Does he get upset easily? Does he do things that make you think, 'OK, that was awkward'?"

Activity

Sample dialogue: "Now I am going to have you complete a survey about yourself and your strengths and weaknesses. When we are done, I will have you share two of your strengths and one area of difficulty or a challenge for you."

Allow the mentors 5-10 minutes to complete the survey (either Worksheet #1 or Worksheet #2). Next have the mentors and the instructor share.

Take home message: After sharing, explain, "Can you imagine if you had to do (insert an area of difficulty here, e.g., math, writing, or spelling) all day long? How would you feel? Would you be angry? Would you be tired? Would you make mistakes?"

Explain this is how the child of focus feels about being social—their area of challenge—all day long.

Sample dialogue: "School is a very social place. We sit by peers in class, we work in groups, we greet them in the halls, we have lunch with others, and we go to recess with others. This is very hard for Joey as his brain struggles with knowing how to be a friend and how to be social with others."

Lastly, talk about when they have those thoughts such as "that was awkward when Joey yelled out in class or sat too close to me in class" and how that is their social radar telling them that Joey did not know the social rule.

Sample dialogue: "When we meet together as a group, you will learn how to help Joey understand those rules and what to say when you notice him saying or doing something that feels 'awkward'; just like a teacher or friend helps you when you are struggling with math or reading and need support."

Mission of the week

End the session with a reminder about confidentiality and that the child of focus will be at the next meeting. Then have the group choose a "Social Squad Mission of the Week." Ideas might be 1) say "hi" to Joey each day when he enters the classroom; 2) invite Joey to eat lunch at your table one time; 3) invite Joey to hang out with you for a few minutes at recess at least one time, etc.

One parting reminder to give students as they prepare to leave, "Joey struggles with social stuff so be a good Social Squad member."

Primary – Social Squad Survey - Worksheet #1 – Page 1

 I FEEL POSITIVE DOING THESE THINGS – Circle the ones you like.

Pets	**Movies**	**Music**

Electronics	**Sports**	**Art**

Doing Math	**Reading**	**Friends**

Telling Jokes	**Cars**	**School**

Games	**Weather**	**Food**

SocialSquad

I FEEL NEGATIVE DOING THESE THINGS – Circle the ones you don't like.

Pets

Movies

Music

Electronics

Sports

Art

Doing Math

Reading

Friends

Telling Jokes

Cars

School

Games

Weather

Food

Intermediate – Social Squad Survey – Worksheet #2

Member:_____ Date:_____

Circle the best answer about you.

More info

1. People at school play with me.
   a. always   b. sometimes   c. never _____

2. I have friends.
   a. always   b. sometimes   c. never _____

3. I'm happy at school.
   a. always   b. sometimes   c. never _____

4. Other children like me.
   a. always   b. sometimes   c. never _____

5. I feel safe with children.
   a. always   b. sometimes   c. never _____

6. I follow adult directions.
   a. always   b. sometimes   c. never _____

7. Changes are ok.
   a. always   b. sometimes   c. never _____

8. I do lots of things with other students.
   a. always   b. sometimes   c. never _____

9. I like to be alone.
   a. always   b. sometimes   c. never _____

10. I want more friends at school.
    a. always   b. sometimes   c. never _____

Lesson 2: First Whole Group

Lesson 2: First Whole Group

*Reminder - prior to this meeting have the child of focus complete the Social Squad Survey. Use Worksheet #1 or #2 depending on ability level (should use same level the rest of the group used in Lesson 1). This is best if completed with an adult who can answer questions or ask questions about the student's responses to gain a good perspective on their responses. If no student is being identified to the other students as needing support, this will be Lesson 1.

Materials for this week's group
- Social Squad Surveys (may have been previously completed in Lesson 1)
- Large paper or white board
- Enough pieces of cardstock (8 ½" x 11") for each person in the group to have one
- Variety of colored markers

Welcome
Sample dialogue: "Welcome to Social Squad. We're all here to learn social skills together."

Discussion
Have each member, including adults, introduce themselves. Review what the purpose for the group is and have each Squad member share one thing they are good at and one thing that is challenging for them (per the surveys done the previous week). Discuss how we all have strengths and challenges, and through this group they will help one another by strengthening their skills to overcome the challenges. In addition, discuss that the interactions among the group members should continue outside the specific group time. You might even give different suggestions each week, known as Squad Missions, for ways they might do this, such as, "try to invite each other to play at least one time at recess between now and our next Squad meeting."

As you are discussing the purpose of the group, let the members know that they need to come up with three to four good rules that everyone agrees would help make them feel more comfortable while sharing and learning together. It may take some prompting by the adult leaders to get them to come up with helpful, realistic rules. Examples of good rules: only one person speaks at a time; give the speaker your attention (may need to define what this looks like); only make positive comments about other members of the group; etc. Write down the rules on the white board or large paper and let students know you will be posting these rules for each future meeting. You can use the "I Am a Great Participator" reward charts (Additional Tools & Resources) for an easy way to motivate members to stick to the rules during future meetings.

Activity
Give each member a piece of cardstock. Tell them they will be making name cards featuring their name and drawing pictures of things they like to do, they are good at, or that they know a lot about. If they are more comfortable writing instead of drawing, that's fine as well. Let them know the cards will be placed in front of them at future meetings so that all Squad members can remember names and what their peers are interested in for conversations, etc.

(The task for this group is to get to know one another. Ensure mentors are engaging the child of focus and complimenting them as they work.)

Once their name cards are completed, have each member hold them up and share with the group. Use this as a time for members to practice asking/answering questions. Remind members you will keep the name cards and have them set up at each meeting. This can easily be a reference for them to ask relevant questions each week about what the other members are interested in. This is especially helpful for students with ASD that may need "friend files" to remember what they can talk about with their new friends.

Mission of the Week

Encourage Squad members to seek each other out during the following week. Let them know you will be asking them at the next Squad meeting about those interactions to make sure they are practicing good social skills.

Squad Report

This week during Social Squad, all of the children met together for the first time. We spent some time getting to know each other. Then we discussed confidentiality and the importance of respecting each other's privacy by not sharing personal information outside of the group time. Students were encouraged to remember that it is expected that they will make connections with each other outside of group time. As we learn new social skills each week, we will remind students to practice these skills together during the week and to give each other gentle social reminders to make good choices. Speaking of good choices, together we created and wrote down rules for how we will treat each other with respect each week during our meetings.

You can expect to receive a Squad Report after each group meeting so that you are aware of what social skills we are working on that week. In the Squad Reports we will also let you know some specific ways you can help practice the new skills at home or in the community. For this week, please take a few minutes to ask your child about the Social Squad. Be sure to ask who is in the group and what they learned about each person today. Challenge them to give you at least one fact about each person in the group, including the adults.

Happy Socializing, from your Squad Leader.

SocialSquad

I FEEL POSITIVE DOING THESE THINGS – Circle the ones you like.

Pets	**Movies**	**Music**

Electronics	**Sports**	**Art**

Doing Math	**Reading**	**Friends**

Telling Jokes	**Cars**	**School**

Games	**Weather**	**Food**

Primary – Social Squad Survey - Worksheet #1 – Page 2

 I FEEL NEGATIVE DOING THESE THINGS – Circle the ones you don't like.

Pets

Movies

Music

Electronics

Sports

Art

Doing Math

Reading

Friends

Telling Jokes

Cars

School

Games

Weather

Food

SocialSquad

Intermediate – Social Squad Survey - Worksheet #2

Member:_____ Date:_____

Circle the best answer about you.

                                                              More info

1. People at school play with me.
   a. always   b. sometimes   c. never _____

2. I have friends.
   a. always   b. sometimes   c. never _____

3. I'm happy at school.
   a. always   b. sometimes   c. never _____

4. Other children like me.
   a. always   b. sometimes   c. never _____

5. I feel safe with children.
   a. always   b. sometimes   c. never _____

6. I follow adult directions.
   a. always   b. sometimes   c. never _____

7. Changes are ok.
   a. always   b. sometimes   c. never _____

8. I do lots of things with other students.
   a. always   b. sometimes   c. never _____

9. I like to be alone.
   a. always   b. sometimes   c. never _____

10. I want more friends at school.
    a. always   b. sometimes   c. never _____

Lesson 3: Parts of Chat

Lesson 3: Parts of Chat

Materials for this week's group

- Parts of Chat worksheets
  - Worksheet #3 is designed to help members stay on track and to gently critique others when they are practicing a chat. Please have one copy for each member.

Note: A variety of additional worksheets are included for you depending on what level of visual supports the members need.

  - Worksheet #4 has pictures paired with words to give primary members ideas for topics to chat about.
  - Worksheet #5 is a written list of possible chat topics for intermediate members.
  - Worksheet #6 is a written list of phrases to begin or end chats.
  - Worksheet #7 gives written sentences with fill in spaces for ways to start a chat and ways to end a chat for intermediate members.
- Pens and pencils for all

Review

Ask how things have been going for everyone since the last Squad meeting. Discuss what interactions they've had with each other outside the group. Prompt them on problem solving any issues of concern that are raised.

Discussion

Introduce students to the idea of a chat session. This will be an important component of future Squad meetings. The idea is to teach students with autism or related issues to have a give-and-take conversation.

Hand out Parts of Chat, Worksheet #3. Describe the "parts of chat" listed in the worksheet. Use the example below to help them understand. A good visual image to use with the students is to describe a successful conversation as being similar to a good volley in a game of Ping-Pong. The ball (or conversation) goes back and forth so that each person gets equal turns. If someone goes off topic unexpectedly, that's hitting a ball that bounces off and is not able to be returned. Also, if the ball just keeps bouncing on the one person's side, then the other person will no longer be able to participate or may not even be interested in participating.

EXAMPLE:
Bob: "Hi Joey."
Joey: "Hi"
Bob: "I played a video game last night. Do you like video games?"
Joey: "Yah! I play Minecraft a lot. Which one do you like best?"
Bob: "Minecraft is my favorite. Well, I gotta go to class. See you later."
Joey: "OK. See ya."

Activity

The adults should model a practice chat and then break the members into pairs and proceed as described below. Challenge them to have a good volley such as in a Ping-Pong game.

If you think your members are going to need extra prompting, you may use any or all of the other worksheets provided for this lesson (see materials list).

Choose two members to do the first chat while others watch and each writes a brief comment (or simple "yes" or "no" for did or did not use that component) on the worksheet in the first row. Once the chat has ended, have members give gentle critiques about how the chat went based on their notes from the Parts of Chat worksheet. Then take turns making sure everyone gets to chat with all the different members while other members take notes on the worksheet. Having them share chats in this way (while critiquing as a group) is the most effective way to give the child of focus a clear picture of good examples versus bad examples rather than having everyone engaged in different chats at the same time.

Please note that while pairs are chatting, adults need to monitor and prompt for appropriate follow through with all the parts of a chat. If the child of focus is struggling with what to say, encourage them with verbal or written prompts. If any students use silly or inappropriate language and interactions, make sure to take advantage of the teachable moment that provides.

For example:
Bob: "Hi, Joey."
Joey: "Hey, Bob. Today is a good day to spit on a friend."
FREEZE

Facilitator should intervene and have Joey look at Bob's expression (prompt Bob to have an appropriate reaction of disgust or embarrassment) to see what the reaction is from Bob. Remind Joey that this is a time to practice serious and respectful conversations. Have them restart the chat and if the silliness continues, give Joey a specific written script to practice during the chat. Feel free to give elaborate praise to those that are making a good effort to use appropriate and respectful chat topics and responses. You may need to go so far as to offer a special treat to those who are making good choices.

Mission of the week
At the end of the Squad meeting, encourage Squad members to have a "chat" with another person before the next Squad meeting. Let them know that we will be discussing this at the opening of the next meeting so they need to come prepared to share what they talked about with another person. You may need to privately encourage mentors to seek out the child of focus to make sure they have a chance to practice one time during the week.

Squad Report

This week during Social Squad we learned how to have a short chat. Members were given the Parts of Chat worksheet and the adults defined for them the process of having a brief conversation with someone. Members were told that having a good conversation was similar to a good volley during a Ping-Pong game. The ball (or conversation) goes back and forth so that each person gets equal turns. If someone goes off topic unexpectedly, that's hitting a ball that bounces off and is not able to be returned. Also, if the ball just keeps bouncing on the one person's side, then the other person will no longer be able to participate or may not even be interested in participating. Please practice having chats with your child and remind them to follow all of the Parts of Chat.

Happy Socializing, from your Squad Leader.

Parts of Chat – Worksheet #3

(P1) Greet a Person	(P2) Respond to Greeting	(P1) Ask Question About a Specific Topic	(P2) Respond to Question and Ask Similar Question – Stay on Topic	(P1) Respond to Question and Then Use Chat Ending	(P2) Respond to Chat Ending

P1 = Person 1
P2 = Person 2

31

Primary – Topics I Can Use for a Chat - Worksheet #4

Sports	Games
Friends	Music
Animals	Books
Cars & Trucks	Electronics
Movies	Food
Weather	School

Intermediate – Topics I Can Use for a Chat - Worksheet #5

Sports	Clothes
Shopping	Games
Animals	Social Media
Friends/Family	Electronic Devices
Movies/TV	Food
Weather	School
Homework	Video Games

Intermediate – Starting and Ending Chats - Worksheet #6

Phrases to Start Chats	Phrases to End Chats
Hi.	It was great seeing you, but I have to go now. Good-bye.
Guess what?	My mom is here so I have to leave now. Good-bye.
What's up?	I have to go to class. See you later.
Hey, how was your weekend?	Got to go. See you later.
Hello.	Well, it's time for me to go now. Good-bye.
It is great to see you.	Hope I see you later, but I have to go now. Good-bye.

How to Start a Chat and Lead to a Topic

Hi.

Guess what?

What's your favorite_____?

Do you like_____?

Do you know_____?

Positive Ways to End a Chat

It was great seeing you, but I have to go now. Good-bye.

My_____ is here so I have to leave now. Good-bye.

I have to go finish_____. Good-bye.

Well, it's time for me to go now. Good-bye.

Hope I see you later, but I have to go now. Good-bye.

Lesson 4: When to Think and When to Talk

Lesson 4: When to Think and When to Talk

Materials for this week's group
- Copy of a thought bubble and a talk bubble (Worksheets #8 and #9)
- Brain filter worksheet (Worksheet #11) for each student.
- Optional – can have an enlarged copy of the Brain Filter worksheet (#11) to use for one of the games.
- Small Post-It notes
- Pens or pencils for all
- Optional: Talk Bubble/Thought Bubble Card (Worksheet #10 folded in half)

Review
Review Parts of Chat from last lesson. Have students pair up and complete a chat with another person.

Discussion
Hold the Talk Bubble over your head and say, "If I was in a cartoon strip, what would this represent?" Repeat with the Thought Bubble. Then talk about the difference between what we say and what we think.

"We think all kinds of different thoughts during the day, but we have something called a filter." Make sure that all Squad members know what a filter is by having them share what they know about filters. Discuss how something enters one side and then the filter retains (or holds back) the items that should not be allowed to come through the other side. We use our brains as a filter to help us know what we can say aloud. When we do this, we think about what we want to say; then we look at who we are with, and then we look around to where we are before we actually talk.

Something we can use to help us with deciding this is the use of a thought bubble and a talk bubble. Show the two bubbles and provide an example (e.g., "for instance, you may think that you do not like your friend's hair, but if you say that out loud, how will that make them feel?"). Have the students determine whether that would make a person happy or sad. Guide them to understand that it would make someone sad, unhappy, etc., and then draw a sad face on the thought bubble paper. Tell them it is okay to think, "I do not like her hair," but not okay to say it. So what can you say instead? Have the group think of ideas. If there are good examples, write one or more down on the talk bubble. Then have the group brainstorm what would their friend's face look like if you said the example instead, and draw the appropriate face on the Talk Bubble paper.

Activity
Play one of these games:

Filtered Thoughts
Place an enlarged copy of the Brain Filter worksheet in the center of the table or attach to a wall/whiteboard. Pass out two Post-It notes to each member along with pens and pencils. Instruct them to write down a separate thought on each Post-It note, but to keep those notes until called on to share. Once all members have written their notes, begin by having one member stand up to share. Instruct them to only do one note/thought at a time and have them initially place the note on the Thought Bubble paper.

Now have a discussion with the group as to whether that thought could make it through the brain filter and be allowed to become a spoken phrase. **OR** should it return to the Thought Bubble and just stay a thought? If the

38

group agrees that the thought could make it safely through the filter and be an appropriate phrase to speak, then they move the Post-It to the Talk Bubble paper.

If they agree that it should not make it through the filter, they leave the Post-It in the Thought Bubble. Encourage members to discuss whether there is a way to alter the thought to help it successfully pass through the filter and become an appropriate spoken phrase. If they can find a more appropriate wording, the original Post-It stays in the Thought Bubble and a new one is written and placed in the Talk Bubble.

You Choose

Have group members stand up in the middle of an open space. Place one bubble on one side of the open area and then place the other bubble on the opposite side of the space. Tell them that you will make a statement and they will have to decide if that is something that should remain a thought or if it's okay to say it out loud. If they think it's okay to say out loud, they move to where the Talk Bubble was placed. If they think it should not be shared out loud, they should move to where the Thought Bubble was placed. Allow members to discuss why they make the choices they make and try to convince others to change if they think they're wrong.

Suggested statements:
- I like macaroni and cheese.
- Macaroni and cheese makes me vomit.
- Jayden's hair is really ugly today.
- Jayden has a great new haircut.
- Brittany smells funny.
- I like George's Magic Cards.

Once you've done this with at least two statements that could be spoken out loud and at least two that should just remain thoughts, step it up a bit. Give them a statement that should remain a thought and once they agree that it should just remain a thought, challenge them to decide if there is an appropriate way to share the thought. For example, the statement could be "I hate having to sit next to Joe at lunch because he smells bad." A better approach would be to not mention that Joe smells bad and just say something like, "I'm going to sit with Ethan at lunch, but let's find each other on the playground at recess. Okay, Joe?"

What Should I Say?

An adult starts this out by holding the Thought Bubble over their head and telling students, "We're going to each take a turn pretending we have a thought about someone or something. It will be a thought we should not share out loud. Then we will change our thought to something positive that could be said in the situation and hold the talk bubble over our head and say something appropriate out loud."

Example:
Adult holding Thought Bubble over their head says, "I think Jared's (another group member—and make sure all understand this is JUST PRETEND) new shirt is really ugly." They then switch and hold up the Talk Bubble and say, "Hey Jared, I see you have a new shirt." Take time to discuss why the bubble thoughts were not okay, and why the spoken words were appropriate. Pass the set of bubbles to the next person in the circle and help them act out and think through the thoughts and words. Let them have fun and laugh about the thoughts as they will likely get pretty silly with some of their comments. Just be sure to remind them that laughing for real in a situation might hurt the other person's feelings so be careful what you practice and when you say and do things.

Note: If you are planning to run your Social Squad group for more than the minimum 8 weeks, plan to incorporate these games at future meetings to use as a review for this vital skill.

Mission of the Week

As you send the members off, tell them this week's challenge is to think prior to saying something. Remind them to decide carefully whether it belongs in a thought bubble or a talk bubble. Optional: give them each a Thought Bubble/Talk Bubble card to put on their desk or notebook as a visual reminder.

Squad Report

This week during our Social Squad meeting, we learned to use our brain as a filter to decide when we should say things and when we should just keep thoughts in our heads. Below is an illustration we used with the members to help them visually process the information. Please see additional instructions below in order to practice this strategy at home with your child. We have also included copies of the Thought Bubble and Talk Bubble for you to use as a visual reminder card for your child.

In future Squad meetings and throughout the school setting, we will be using verbal prompts such as "Thought bubble or talk bubble?"; "Is that something to say or just keep in your thought bubble?"; or simply "Thought bubble." These prompts will remind students to think and process information before they talk or blurt out.

Happy Socializing, from your Squad Leader.

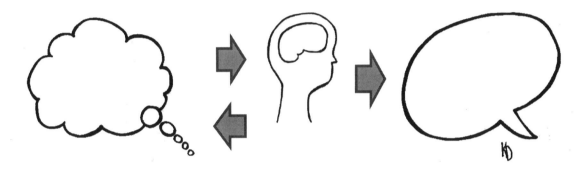

1) Thoughts come into your head.
2) Your brain filter decides if that can be spoken or needs to remain a thought.
3) Sometimes the brain filter can help you change the thoughts into words that can be spoken.

Thought Bubble - Worksheet #8

Thought Bubble/Talk Bubble Card – Worksheet #10

Brain Filter - Worksheet #11

Use your brain to filter thoughts so that appropriate words come out when you talk.

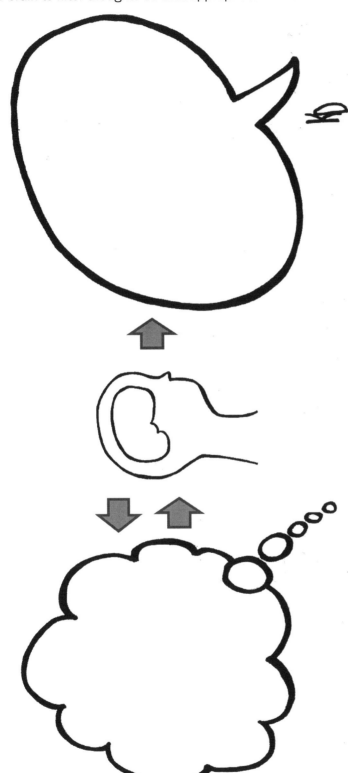

Thoughts come into your head.

2) Your brain filter decides if that can be spoken or needs to remain a thought.

3) Sometimes the brain filter can help you change the thoughts into words that can be spoken.

Lesson 5: Flip the Switch

Lesson 5: Flip the Switch

Materials for this week's group

- Flip the Switch Card folded in half (Worksheet #12)
- Small index cards (enough for two for each member)
- Pencils for all

Review

Have students review how the last week went. Did they practice using their brain filter? Discuss any areas of concern and help problem solve ways to handle them in the future. Next practice a chat in pairs.

Discussion

Tell Squad members that today we will be talking about things people say and do that can negatively affect our thoughts and feelings. Using the Flip the Switch Card (Worksheet #12) write down (on the negative side) things people say that give us sad or upset thoughts (e.g., dog died, someone took the ball from us at recess, mom and dad said to turn off our video game). Next discuss what would be positive thoughts. Write down a list of positive thoughts, on the positive side of the paper (e.g., made a new friend, favorite video game, a funny movie, a fun event with family). Discuss how if we get stuck or focused only on the negative thoughts, we feel sad or upset more often. Now discuss that there is a bright side. Tell them they can control and change these thoughts by moving them from the negative side to the positive side with a technique called "flip the switch." This technique often uses words such as *but, however,* and *instead,* etc. Discuss that when we flip the switch, it helps get rid of the negative thoughts and allows the positive thoughts to come back in. Teachers can also model this by turning off the lights in the room and saying a negative thought and then flipping on the light switch while saying a positive thought, to again model how it can change our perspective.

Activity

Now model how to do this using a small index card. Write or draw a negative thought, (e.g., "I have no friends.") Then model flipping the switch by using the words listed above (*but, however, instead*), and write a positive thought on the other side of the card (e.g., "However, I am in a Social Squad and making new friends in this group.") Discuss how these thoughts give us different feelings, and we can control them by focusing on the positive thoughts and not getting stuck on the negative ones.

Next give each member an index card and have them write or draw a negative thought. Then tell them to flip the switch (turning over the card) and write or draw a positive thought using the words provided (*but, however, instead*). This may be very hard for some students so make sure you are walking around and assisting them in how to flip the switch. At first you may need to write down a positive thought for them. Have the members share their cards and flip the switch.

Mission of the Week

Before members leave, encourage them to notice when they are having negative thoughts and practice flipping the switch to the positive ones. Once they flip the switch, have them notice how they feel when they are able to focus on positive thoughts. Let members know these will be shared next week to see who was able to flip the switch and how they did it.

Squad Report

This week during Social Squad, we learned a concept called "Flip the Switch." We talked about negative thoughts and positive thoughts. And we practiced changing our negative thoughts into positive thoughts. We did this by giving them each a small index card and asking them to write or draw a negative thought, (e.g., "I have no friends.") Then we modeled flipping the switch by using the words *but, however, instead*, and then wrote a positive thought on the other side of the card (e.g., "However, I am in a Social Squad and making new friends in this group.") We then discussed how these thoughts give us different feelings, and we can control them by focusing on the positive thoughts and not getting stuck on the negative ones.

Please practice at home by helping your child flip the switch when they are stuck on only negative thoughts. A good time to do this is when they come home from school and only have negative things to say. Parents can say, "Wow! That is a lot of negative thoughts. Let's flip the switch and tell me one okay or good thing that happened at school." Doing this daily will help the child learn to do this naturally on their own, and an overall change in how they see the world will most likely be the result—a much more positive place for all.

Happy Socializing, from your Squad Leader.

Flip the Switch Card – Worksheet #12

Lesson 6: I Think/You Think

Lesson 6: I Think/You Think

Materials for this week's group
- One copy for each member of the "I Think/You Think" worksheet (Worksheet #13)
- Pens or pencils for all
- About three small objects, such as a cup, a stapler, a pair of scissors, etc.
- Three or four pieces of paper with different scenarios written on them that can be acted out quickly (i.e., two students greet each other or someone gives another person a piece of candy, etc.)
- Three or four pieces of paper with expressions written on them (i.e., "That's cool!" or "Hey there.")

Review
How was the last week? Did you meet the challenge from last week's group? Are there any concerns that anyone has?

Discussion/Activity
Pass out the worksheets and pens/pencils to each member. Tell them you will now be placing an object in the middle of the table and you want them not to say anything out loud to anyone about what they see. Tell them that once they've looked at the object for 10-20 seconds, you want them to write down what their first thought is when they see it. They will be writing their answer in the first "I think" space on their worksheet. They just need to write a word or two, not a whole sentence. Then put one of the three previously chosen objects in the middle of the table.

For this example, we will say that you placed the cup in the middle of the table. Once everyone has something written in their first "I think" space, begin asking them to each share what they wrote when they saw the cup. They will probably say more than the one or two words they wrote down. It is fine for them to elaborate verbally. Some thoughts you will probably get about the cup might be: "It makes me thirsty." "I wish I had a cup full of fruit juice." "Drinking too much liquid makes me need to use the bathroom." "My grandma has cups like that at her house." Have members write at least one other person's thought in the first "You think" space on the worksheet.

Once everyone has shared what they wrote, point out the similarities and differences in what they each thought even though they were each looking at exactly the same object at the same time. Tell them this is called "personal perspective" and everyone has a personal perspective on everything they see and hear around them. Not everyone sees and hears things and has the same reaction as the people around them. Often their thoughts will be similar, but sometimes they are completely different.

Continue this activity with one or two more objects. Be aware of whether the child of focus understands the concept of "personal perspective" and relate that it is important to never assume that you know what another person is thinking. Share that this is one of those areas that is not black and white and may not seem logical to them. If this is an area that creates challenging behaviors for them, use this opportunity to have Social Squad members share coping strategies for frustration and confusion.

Next, do this activity with words and/or actions. Use your prewritten scenarios or phrases to help prompt them. Use the same format of having them write down their first thoughts in the "I think" space and then when everyone shares, they can write down at least one other person's thoughts in the "You think" space.

Discuss how people have "personal perspectives" about words and actions just like they do with objects. Now you're in the area that most likely impacts the child of focus. Use this time to talk about being aware that others may not understand when we say or do certain things. We may mean one thing, and they might "take it wrong."

Mission of the Week

As you send the children off, remind them this week's challenge is to be aware that others have different thoughts than they do about lots of things. Have them think about this and be prepared to come back and share what they notice over the next week in regard to "personal perspectives."

Squad Report

This week during our Squad meeting we learned that people have different perspectives. Sometimes this is called perspective taking. We demonstrated this concept by doing the following activity.

Students were given worksheets with "I Think/You Think" written on them. Items were placed in the middle of the table (one at a time), and students were asked to write what the item made them think in the "I Think" column. They then took turns sharing their answers, and while they shared, notes were made in the "You Think" column as to what the item made other people think.

Once everyone had shared what they wrote, the adult pointed out the similarities and differences in what they each thought even though they were each looking at exactly the same object at the same time. They were told this is called "personal perspective," and everyone has a personal perspective on everything that they see and hear around them. Not everyone sees and hears things in the same way or has the same reaction as the people around them. Often their thoughts will be similar, but sometimes they are completely different.

We also did this activity with words and/or actions. We discussed how people have "personal perspectives" about words and actions just like they do with objects. We used this time to talk about being aware that others may not understand when we say or do certain things. We may mean one thing, and they might "take it wrong."

We encourage you to practice this activity with your child. Use unique opportunities to point out different people's perspectives to your child. This concept is often a challenge for children with Autism Spectrum Disorders. It is important for them to be aware that other people do not always think about something in the same way that they do. It is good for them to know that other people need to be told what they are thinking if it is different than their own thoughts. We are working to help other people interacting with your child to understand that their view may cause them to have what might appear to be inappropriate reactions, when in fact it is just a different perspective. We will be repeating these concepts throughout the course of the Social Squad.

Happy Socializing, from your Squad Leader.

I Think/You Think - Worksheet #13

1) I think:	1) You think:

2) I think:	2) You think:

3) I think:	3) You think:

4) I think:	4) You think:

Lesson 7: My Personal Universe

Lesson 7: My Personal Universe

NOTE: This lesson may need to be split into two sessions if the material needs to be covered in depth for the benefit of the child of focus.

Materials for this week's group
- Draw a large set of circles on the whiteboard and label it Personal Universe (use Worksheet #14 as a model).
- Small Post-Its
- Pens or pencils for all
- Copies of the Personal Universe worksheet (Worksheet #14) to pass out to each member at the end of group

Review
Have students review how the last week went. Discuss any areas of concern and help problem solve ways to handle that now or in the future.

Discussion
"Let's look at the circles on the board. Please understand that this is NOT a target." Point to the Personal Universe you have drawn on the board. "Let's imagine that these rings represent your personal universe and you are at the center." Write *me* in the center. Next ask, "What group of people is closest to you in your life?" They should answer, "family," and you write the word *family* in the ring closest to *me* in the center. Then you can briefly discuss who family includes. (Remember to allow that family may include guardians or special people that are responsible for them; they don't have to be physically related.)

Moving to the next ring, ask Squad members what the name is for the group of people that is next in their personal universe. The answer should be "friends," and this should be written in the ring next to *family*. Have a discussion to help them identify what makes a person a friend. The answers could include any variation on "someone you hang out with, call on the phone, play with at recess or after school, and share fun memories with…" Make a written list with them about what they consider to be criteria for what qualifies a person as a friend (you will do the same for acquaintances) so that you can use this during the activity portion of the meeting. Making a written list of these characteristics is especially useful in helping members with autism understand the subtle differences between friends and acquaintances and the different ways you should interact with these two groups of people.

The next ring is intended to be identified as "acquaintances," but most elementary (and some older) students will struggle slightly about the concept of acquaintances. Therefore, it is sometimes helpful to skip over this ring initially and come back to it after talking about the next ring which is "strangers."

Ask members what name is given to the group of people that are the farthest from their inner circle. Their answer should be "strangers." As you write the word in the last circle, have a discussion about what makes a person a stranger. Discuss that you may actually know where they live (neighbor) and/or what their name is (may be a clerk wearing a name badge), but you don't really know them personally. Please be sure to note that a stranger does not always mean a bad, wicked, or scary person. They are just someone you don't know, and you need to be careful about talking with strangers.

Now you can go back and discuss acquaintances and relate that they are sort of in between friends and strangers. You know their name and a little bit about them, but you never really hang out with them because you don't know them well yet. They could be a friend of a friend, a neighbor you greet on a regular basis, the clerk at the grocery store you say "hi" to every week, an adult or student at your school that you are aware of but don't spend time with, etc. Acquaintances are people you know a little bit so they aren't truly strangers, but you don't spend as much time with them as you do your friends. Discuss that every friend was once a stranger, then an acquaintance, and eventually became a friend.

Now say, "Since we've been talking about who is in your universe, let's move on to talk more about how you talk to the different people in the different areas. For instance, what are things you might say to people that are family? Are they the same things you would say to people that are in the friend group? How about people in the acquaintance group and stranger group?" Engage them in a discussion of what things are appropriate to say to people in the different groups. It's also good to discuss when you can have these conversations. For example, it's okay to ask a friend to come to your house to visit but not when the teacher is in the middle of a lesson at school.

You may need to explain again that not all strangers are dangerous people. Remind them that a store clerk or usher at the theater are strangers to them, but they are people you can talk to briefly. It's okay to say "hello" and ask questions related to their job that might help you (such as "do you know which aisle has the soup?"), but that you would not share personal information with these people or ask them questions about themselves.

Activity

Give each Squad member two small Post-Its and a pen or pencil. Instruct them to each write one name on each Post-It and hold them until called on to share. Make sure the adults in the group do this activity as well. When everyone has had a chance to write down names, ask for a volunteer to start sharing.

Have the member stand up and read off the first name from one of their Post-Its. Now each person in the group takes a turn asking a question about how the person knows the person on the Post-It. For example: "How much time do you spend with this person?" "Do you know this person's favorite color, food, etc.?" "Do you know what this person's hobbies are?" Basically, you want the members to identify whether this person is a family member, friend, acquaintance, or stranger of the Squad member who wrote the name. Once a unanimous decision is reached as to what category this person belongs in, the member then puts the Post-It on that area of the Personal Universe.

Have the member read their second name and allow all to ask questions again in order to categorize the name. Have each Squad member do this activity with the names they've written. This is a great teaching time for the child of focus in your group to be learning what a true friend is and how to tell if a person is your friend and can be trusted, etc. It also is a time when they will begin learning more about what you say and do with different people and that not all people can be treated with the same level of sharing, etc.

Mission of the Week

Hand out the Personal Universe (worksheet #14) as homework for them to work on as their challenge during the next week. Instruct them to fill in specific names of people that fit into each group in their own lives. Encourage them to share the filled-in universe with someone outside the group and to discuss with them how they interact with the different people in the different rings. Also encourage members to make contact with each other on the playground or lunchroom during the week.

Squad Report

During this week's Squad meeting we talked about the concept of being the center of our own universe. We used a larger version of the image below to help illustrate that an individual is the center. The next closest group of people is family or people you live with. Next are friends and we clearly define that friends are people you know quite a bit about and you choose to spend time doing activities together. Acquaintances are people that you may know. In fact, you may know their names and a little bit about them, but you don't really spend much time interacting or playing with them. These may be classmates. We remind students that while classmates or other groups of people we are involved in together may be friendly to one another, that connection does not automatically make them friends.

Finally, we discussed strangers. Strangers are the people furthest from your center and they are the people you really do not know. We stress that strangers are not always dangerous people, but they are people you know nothing about, and you need to be careful about talking to them.

WHO ARE THE PEOPLE I KNOW?

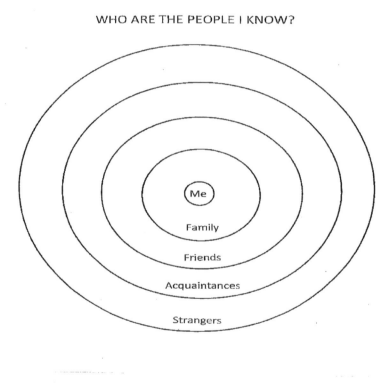

Intellectual Property of Nicole Bain, PhD and Kathie Davis

We have sent a large version of this sheet home with your child. Please take a few minutes to help your child fill in actual names of people that fit into the different circles and have them bring it back to group next week. In next week's meeting, we will be discussing these groups and what types of things you should or should not say or do with the different groups of people.

Happy Socializing, from your Squad Leader.

WHO ARE THE PEOPLE I KNOW?

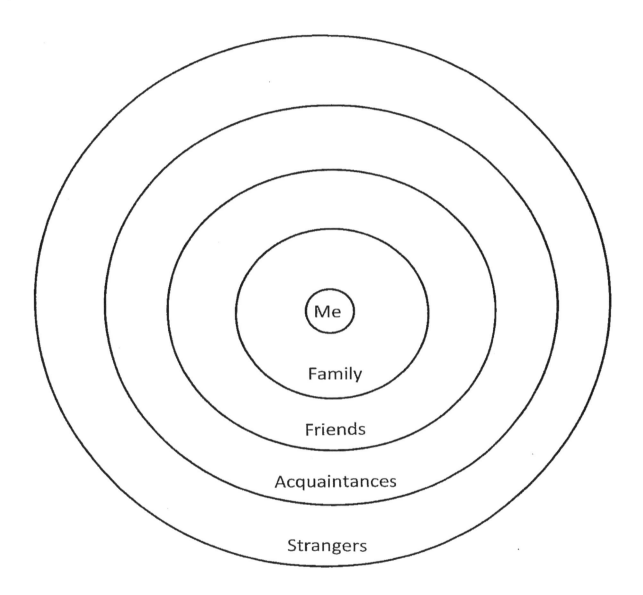

Lesson 8: Talking Tips

Lesson 8: Talking Tips

Materials for this week's group

- One copy of the Personal Universe worksheet (Worksheet #14—from Lesson 7)
- Each student should have brought back their filled in copies of the Personal Universe worksheet from last week's Mission of the Week.
- Enough copies of the Talking Tips worksheet (Worksheet #15) for each member
- One copy of the example worksheet (Worksheet #16) for reference on how to use #15
- Pens or pencils for all
- A game, such as Apples to Apples, WHOONU, or Jenga with colored cards to correlate with colored dots on the Jenga pieces (see directions below).

Review

Have students review how the last week went. Discuss any areas of concern and help problem solve ways to handle that now or in the future.

Discussion

After you review who is in your universe, move on to talk more about how you talk to the different people in the different parts of your universe. Pass out the copies of the Talking Tips worksheet (Worksheet #15) to each member and encourage them to fill these in as they are having the discussion. You can use the example sheet (Worksheet #16) for ideas to prompt them as to what is appropriate. Remind members what you discussed last week about what's appropriate to say to different people. Talk about what things you might say to people who are family. Are they the same things you would say to people who are friends? How about people in the acquaintance group and stranger group? Engage members in a discussion of what things are appropriate to say to people in the different groups. It's also good to discuss when you can have these conversations. For example, it's okay to ask a friend to come over to your house to visit, but it's not okay to ask when the teacher is in the middle of a lesson at school.

Make sure that members have taken notes on their worksheets in order to use them in real life as a reminder about appropriate conversations with the different people in their lives.

Activity

Play one of the suggested board games above.

Directions for Jenga with colored dots:

- Stack the Jenga pieces in the center of the table (per typical Jenga game instructions).
- Write on white board or paper on table top the game instructions for what to do if you successfully remove a specific colored Jenga piece. You can make them up as a group, but here are some examples:
  o Blue = Tell about a time when you were embarrassed; how did you handle it?
  o Red = Tell about a time when you were angry; how did you handle it?
  o Yellow = Tell about a time when you were excited about something; how did you handle it?
  o Green = Tell about a time you were sad; how did you handle it?

OR

- o Blue = Ask the person to your left what they are doing after school today.
- o Red = Tell the person to your right what you are doing after school today.
- o Yellow = Tell the person across from you something about your family.
- o Green = Ask the person across from you about their family.

OR

Get creative and make up any "color directions" that apply to the needs of the group.

Mission of the Week

As you send the members off, tell them this week's challenge is to share their Talking Tips paper with a teacher, parent, or other adult in their life. Encourage them to use the worksheet as a personal reminder about when and where and who to say specific things to throughout the week. Also, remind them that the purpose of the group is to be supportive of each other, so ask them to make sure they make contact with each other at some point during the next week.

Squad Report

During our Squad meeting this week we reviewed the Personal Universe worksheets from last week. We then transferred information from each student's filled in Personal Universe worksheets onto a Talking Tips worksheet. These worksheets helped us define what category individual people belong to: family, friend, acquaintance, or stranger. We worked together to decide what topics could be discussed with the different groups. The options were "appropriate topics to discuss with this group," "when it's appropriate to have those discussions," and "NOT appropriate topics to discuss with this group."

Ask your child to share their worksheet with you and have a discussion about what they learned in group this week. You may expand the discussion to include actions not just topics. Peers were reminded to help give gentle prompts to one another outside of group time if they feel a person needs to remember what is okay to say to different people and when it's okay to say those things.

Happy Socializing, from your Squad Leader.

SocialSquad

Who, What, and When

PERSON	WHO THEY ARE	THESE ARE APPROPRIATE TOPICS TO DISCUSS WITH THIS GROUP OF PEOPLE	I CAN DISCUSS APPROPRIATE TOPICS WHEN	THESE ARE <u>NOT</u> APPROPRIATE TOPICS TO DISCUSS WITH THIS GROUP OF PEOPLE
Family Member				
Friend				
Acquaintance				
Stranger				

Example Copy - Talking Tips - Worksheet #16

Who, What, and When

PERSON	WHO THEY ARE	THESE ARE APPROPRIATE TOPICS TO DISCUSS WITH THIS GROUP OF PEOPLE	I CAN DISCUSS APPROPRIATE TOPICS WHEN	THESE ARE <u>NOT</u> APPROPRIATE TOPICS TO DISCUSS WITH THIS GROUP OF PEOPLE
Family Member	my sister Dana my sister Jan my dad my mom	Where we are going on vacation this year What grade I got on a test How much money our family spent on a new T.V.	In the car on the way to or from school In our home when we don't have visitors	Safe secrets friends share with me, such as what boy they like or what they think about another friend
Friend	Ashleigh Carolyn Marta	What clothes we each like to wear What boy we think is really cute Who we wish would ask us to sit with them at lunch	On the phone after school or on the weekend During lunch or recess At each other's homes	How much money my dad or mom gets paid for their job
Acquaintance	Carolyn's brother Marta's friend from her old school	What kind of music they listen to What are their favorite movies	During lunch or recess Or when I see them at someone's home or in the community	Maybe not tell them my phone number or home address until they become my friend or I think I'm ready to start spending more time with them
Stranger	Checker at the grocery store Person sitting in the doctor's office waiting room UPS delivery person	Only a brief "hello" or "have a nice day"	When I see them in public	I NEVER tell a stranger my phone number, address, or other personal info unless my parent is with me and says it's okay (i.e. I'm ordering something to be delivered to my home)

Lesson 9: Connect the Thoughts

Lesson 9: Connect the Thoughts

Materials for this week's group
- Connect the Thoughts blank worksheet (Worksheet #17)
- Connect the Thoughts example (Worksheet #18)
- Blank white paper or a white board and dry erase marker
- Pens or pencils for all

Review
How was the last week? Did you meet the challenge from last week's group? Are there any concerns that anyone has? Next complete a chat session to continue the use of these skills.

Discussion/Activity
At the end of the chat introduce the idea of staying on one topic or "Connecting the Thoughts." Ask members to share the topics they discussed in their chats and write each one down on a blank piece of paper or a white board. Lead into the Activity by stating the importance of staying on the topic throughout the chat to make sure the other Squad member gets a clear picture of what you are discussing.

Start a conversation with a Squad member. Choose a topic (e.g., school, weather, foods, or animals) and go back and forth a few times in a chat format. Next, say a comment about a completely unrelated topic (such as last summer's vacation). Pause and see the group's reaction. Discuss whether that was on topic or off topic? Describe how when we have a conversation about a topic, we are creating a "picture" or "story" that is connected about that topic; when someone adds a comment that is unrelated, it does not fit that picture or story.

Next pass out the Connect the Thoughts worksheet (worksheet #17). Sitting in a circle, see how long the group can connect the thoughts (use a blank sheet of paper or the white board to track how many thoughts were connected). Next have the group divide into pairs and see what group can connect the thoughts the longest.

Next Level: teach members ways to successfully transition from one topic of thoughts to a new topic. For example, if the discussion is about snow, a successful transition to dogs would be "My dog loves the snow. Do you have a dog?" This can also be modeled on the Connect the Thought worksheet or the white board. Complete the activity above using this new concept.

Mission of the Week
During the next week, have small chats with group members. Make sure that your thoughts are connected to the chat. If you notice someone changes the topic unexpectedly, you can politely say, "Was that thought connected?" or "Remember, we need to connect our thoughts." This can also be done with family members or people in the school community.

SocialSquad

Squad Report

This week during Social Squad, we learned how to make sure our thoughts are connected. We shared the attached Connect the Thoughts worksheet and discussed that when we keep our thoughts connected, it creates a mental "picture" or "story" so others can follow the path and see the big picture of what we are talking about. We discussed that if someone makes a comment that is not connected, it confuses the "picture" or "story" we are creating together.

We practiced this a few times and then left members with the challenge to have chats with other group members or their family outside of our formal meeting time. We suggested that if they notice someone changes the topic unexpectedly, they could politely say, "Was that thought connected?" or "Remember, we need to connect our thoughts." Please feel free to practice this with your child on the blank sheet provided.

Happy Socializing, from your Squad Leader.

Connect the Thoughts - Worksheet #17

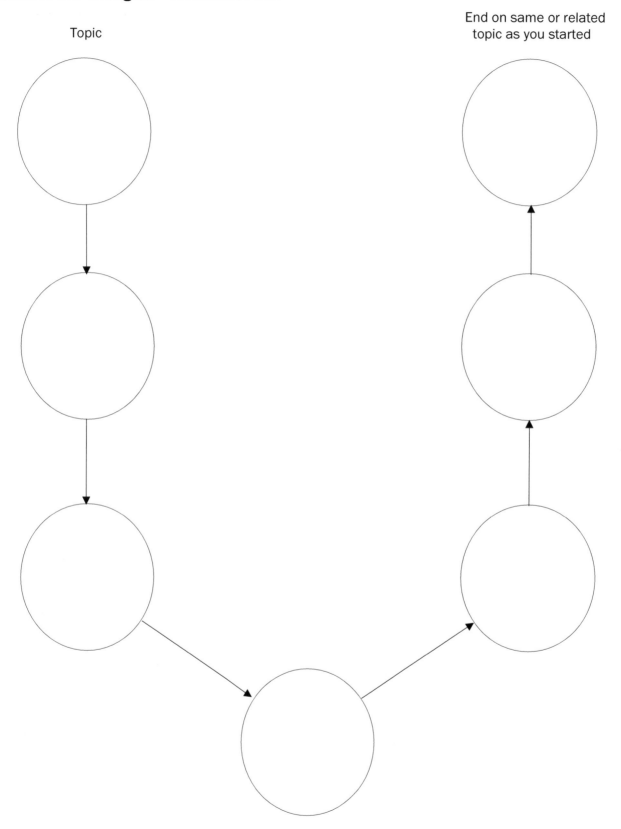

Topic

End on same or related
topic as you started

72

SocialSquad

Example Connect the Thoughts – Worksheet #18

Topic

End on same or related topic as you started

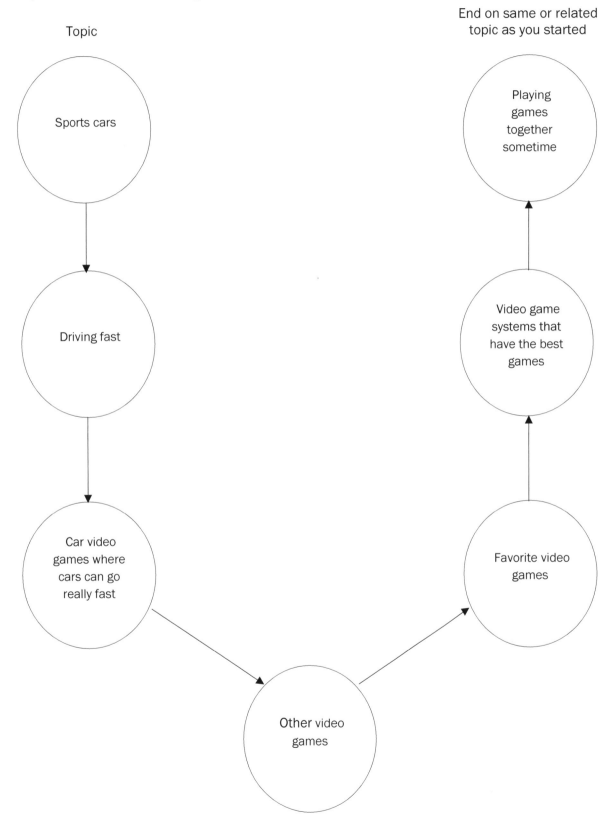

Sports cars

Driving fast

Car video games where cars can go really fast

Other video games

Favorite video games

Video game systems that have the best games

Playing games together sometime

73

Lesson 10: Positive or Negative Behavior?

Lesson 10: Positive or Negative Behavior?

Materials for this week's group

- One copy of the Positive or Negative worksheet (Worksheet #19) for each Social Squad Member. (This is sometimes also referred to as Expected or Unexpected Behavior.)
- Pens or pencils for all

Review

Have students review how the last week went. Discuss any areas of concern and help problem solve ways to handle that now or in the future.

Discussion

Tell Squad members that today we will be talking about things that people say and do and discussing how those words and actions might make other people feel. Give them an example of a time when someone said something to you that was positive and made you feel good. (Example: "Yesterday my friend I've had for many years told me she's really glad that we still spend a lot of time together. This made me feel really great.") Next, give an example of a time when someone said something negative, and it made you feel uncomfortable. (Example: "This morning, when I asked a co-worker if she liked my hair, she told me it is ugly. I was not expecting this, and my feelings were hurt. That was not cool.") Briefly discuss a more polite comment the person could have made if she hadn't liked your hair. This is a great time to remind members to use their "filter" which they learned about in Lesson 4.

Now give a couple of examples of actions that someone might do that would be positive and negative. (Example of positive: "I dropped a book when I was walking down the hallway, and a student I didn't know picked it up for me. That was really kind. I like it when people do cool things like that." Example of negative: "When I was eating my lunch yesterday, another person reached over and took some of my grapes without saying anything. I was not expecting anything like that to happen. It was totally rude.") Discuss how the other person might have avoided making you feel uncomfortable.

Activity

Pass out the Positive or Negative worksheet (Worksheet #19) and pens/pencils for each member. Give an example of a comment someone might make or an action they might take. Have the group decide whether that comment or action would belong on the Positive or Negative side of the paper. Once the group decides, they can write it in the appropriate column. Next have them discuss how the comment or action might make someone feel and instruct them to write the answer in the corresponding column.

Go around the table and have each member share an example of either a comment or action, and discuss as a group whether it's positive or negative and have them write down the answers. Continue as long as time allows or until all members have shared at least once.

An alternative would be to use one copy of the worksheet for one person to do all the writing, either directly at the table, taped on the wall, or best of all, displayed on an overhead for everyone to be able to see.

Mission of the Week

Before students leave, encourage them to be thinking about their words and actions during the next week. Tell them you expect them to work on making sure that their own words and actions are not causing others to be uncomfortable or even sad. Remind them of the Thought and Talk Bubble lesson and to use their filters to keep thoughts or actions in the brain (filter) instead of acting on those thoughts when they shouldn't be allowed through the filter.

Squad Report

This week during our Squad meeting we discussed Positive and Negative behavior, sometimes referred to as Expected or Unexpected behavior. Together, Squad members determined whether certain behaviors would be considered positive or negative and how those behaviors might make another person feel if you did them to them or in front of them. We then discussed how making a person feel positive or negative might then impact how you feel. We further discussed that it is each individual person's job to make other people feel comfortable around them. That's why it is important to know how our specific behaviors might impact others.

Please continue this ongoing discussion with your child. We have sent home a blank sheet of the paperwork we used today to process positive and negative behavior. Feel free to use this at home to help process misunderstandings between your child and other individuals or to help prepare them for upcoming activities that you anticipate may be challenging for them.

Happy Socializing, from your Squad Leader.

Positive or Negative – Worksheet #19

I Say or Do	Other Person Feels	Then I Feel	Is This Positive or Negative?	How Can I Fix Negative?

Lesson 11: Sensory Awareness

Lesson 11: Sensory Awareness

Materials for this week's group
- Sensory items listed below in the activity section

Review
Have students review how the last week went. Discuss any areas of concern and help problem solve ways to handle that now or in the future.

Discussion
Over the last several weeks we have been talking about perspective taking and how our behavior affects others. Let's look more at different behaviors that we each have and reasons for those behaviors. We are going to talk about our senses. Name a few of the senses we all have (e.g., taste, smell, touch, sight, and hearing). Give an example of a situation where someone might have an aversive sensory reaction (e.g., what happens when you are in class and the fire alarm goes off?). Have students share their reactions to some or all of the following:

(Brainstorm all the different senses and items that are unpleasant to each child.)
Taste—possibly candy, spicy foods, textures of foods;
Smell—possibly flowers, burnt toast, sour milk, a person's breath;
Touch—possibly clothing, hugs, how close others sit next to you;
Sight—possibly bright lights, no lights, sunlight, too many items in a room;
Hearing—possibly music, nails on a chalk board, people chewing.

Next discuss the different senses and items that are pleasant to each child. After each person has shared what they enjoy within each sense and what they cannot tolerate, discuss how each person differs in how their senses tolerate things. Now discuss reactions to unpleasant and pleasant sensory items and share how each person has a different reaction. Sometimes when we are overwhelmed by a sense, we just want to make the sensory item stop. Finally, brainstorm ways to help others cope better when overwhelmed by sensory items.

Activity
Using items from the list below have each student taste, smell, touch, see, or hear the different items per the instructions. Once each student has had a turn with each sense and the related items, have them share what it felt like and if they enjoyed the items or felt overwhelmed by them.

Taste: sour candy or spicy candy—have each child hold the candy in their mouths for 15 seconds.
Smell: candle, room deodorizer, perfume—have each child smell the item for 15 seconds.
Touch: burlap sack or other scratchy material—have each child touch it for 15 seconds.
Sight: dark and light—have a student cover their eyes using their hands or a blindfold; then have them uncover their eyes and try not to blink for 15 seconds.
Hearing: a bell, loud music—have a person listen to the music while another person is trying to talk to them.

Mission of the Week
As you send the children off, tell them this week's challenge is to think of all the reactions they have to different sensory experiences. Remember things they do to avoid or seek out certain senses and come back

ready to share these experiences next week. Also, if a student has already identified a strong negative reaction to something sensory, encourage the other members to help them when they encounter those things outside of group time. You might also encourage the other group members to avoid using items around that member if they think it might create a strong reaction.

Squad Report

This week during our Squad meeting we discussed our senses. We discussed how we each register sensory issues differently. We addressed taste, smell, touch, sight, and hearing. We experienced different sensory items and talked about how different people felt about the different items. Throughout the activity we discussed how important it is to understand how other people are impacted by sensory issues. We talked about what we could do to support someone who may have strong reactions to different sensory issues.

If your child exhibits or reports strong reactions to sensory input, please help support them in learning how to advocate for themselves appropriately with others about those issues. You might also help your child find ways to cope with those issues for those times when sensory input will be unavoidable.

Happy Socializing, from your Squad Leader.

Lesson 12: Joining a Group

Lesson 12: Joining a Group

Materials for this week's group

- Notepad or white board
- Enough copies of the Look Fors worksheet (Worksheet #20) for each member
- Pens or pencils for all

Review

Have students review how the last week went. Discuss any areas of concern and help problem solve ways to handle that now or in the future.

Discussion

Discuss ways that we interact with or engage others at school. For instance, we can approach one person who is sitting or standing by themselves or we can walk up to a group of students who are sitting or standing together. Remind the group members that we have discussed how to have a chat with one person and then have the members share if they think approaching a group of peers is different than just approaching one person standing or sitting alone.

Ideas to discuss:
- What to do if they are walking up to a group that is already talking about a specific topic?
- What to do when approaching a group of peers that are your friends versus a group that are acquaintances?

Next pass out the Look Fors worksheet (Worksheet #20). Instruct students to fill in their individual sheets as they share what are important things/actions when joining a group:
- What do they listen for when joining a group?
- What do they look for?
- How close do they stand to the others?

Activity

Once a list has been created, use this list to role-play joining a group. Have all the members gather together and then have a peer mentor join the group. After this, have them explain how they knew what to do. What did they listen for? What did they look for? Have each member join the group with the child of focus joining the group last. Coach them as needed as to what to listen for and what to look for when approaching the group. After each person has joined the group, have them share how it went. What was easy and what was difficult for them?

Mission of the Week

Challenge each member to join a group during the next week. Remind them to use their Look Fors when joining the group. Encourage the peer mentors to also invite the child of focus to join a group. Remind them they will be expected to share how it went the following week in group.

SocialSquad

Squad Report

During this week's Squad meeting, we discussed how to join a group of people on the playground, in the lunchroom, etc. We shared how to know when it's okay to join a group and how to know when it's okay to begin talking once you've joined the group. Your child may bring home their copy of the tip sheet we filled in as a group. We are also sending a blank copy of the sheet that may be helpful for you to use with your child before going on an outing that may require some preparation ahead of time.

Happy Socializing, from your Squad Leader.

Look Fors When Joining a Group - Worksheet #20

Look Fors When Joining a Group

	Look	Listen
What is the topic?		
How close are people standing in the group?		
Was there a pause in the conversation?		
What was the ending statement?		
Other observations?		

Lesson 13: BIG DEAL or little deal

Lesson 13: BIG DEAL or little deal

Materials for this week's group
- Make four columns on white board. Column one should be titled *BIG DEAL* and column three should be titled *little deal*. Columns two and four will be labeled and filled in after the activity begins.

Example:

BIG DEAL	Appropriate Response	little deal	Appropriate Response

- Scenario cards (Worksheet #21) – these need to be printed and cut out ahead of time and could be laminated for durability; OR you could write them on Post-It notes. Blanks are available to add your own scenarios. This is especially useful if there are specific scenarios you need to work on with a child.
- One BIG DEAL or little deal worksheet (Worksheet #22) for each Squad member.

Review
Have students review how the last week went. Did they practice joining a group? How did that work out for them? Discuss any areas of concern and help problem solve ways to handle that now or in the future.

Discussion
Discuss that in the last several weeks we've been learning about our own emotions or feelings and how other people might feel differently about the same thing. We've also talked about how our actions or reactions to things might make people feel differently than we expect them to feel. Sometimes our reactions don't match what's happening, and this confuses people.

Today we're going to learn about BIG DEAL or little deal. The idea is that some things are a BIG DEAL, or big problem, and they need to be taken care of right away. But some things are just a little deal or a little problem and can probably just be ignored, at least for now. Share that even if something is a BIG DEAL, you still need to calmly seek help to fix the problem and not make it a bigger problem by yelling, raging, or having a tantrum.

Activity
Point out columns one and three on the board. Tell members, "You can see that one is for BIG DEAL and one is for little deal." Give each member a scenario card that was prepared ahead of time.

Instruct members that each person will get to take a turn to share what is written on their scenario card and then the group will discuss together whether that is a BIG DEAL or a little deal. Once the group agrees what column the scenario belongs in (and this may take some adult intervention to come to an appropriate decision), the member can then tape or place their scenario in the appropriate column. Go around the group until all scenarios have been shared and placed on the white board.

Now write "Appropriate Response" in both of the two remaining columns. Next challenge the members to help come up with appropriate responses to the scenarios taped on the board. Once they've agreed on an appropriate decision, write that on the board in the "Appropriate Response" column to the right of the scenario. You may need to have some prewritten responses to choose from for younger children or those unable to generate ideas on their own.

Have patience and be aware that this activity may be quite challenging for the child of focus who struggles with emotion regulation and/or rigid social thinking. Once this lesson is taught, BIG DEAL or little deal language should be shared with all people involved with supporting this person in order to generalize the lesson.

Mission of the Week

Pass out a BIG DEAL or little deal worksheet to each member. Tell them you would like them to share this with an adult this week and talk about what things are a BIG DEAL and what things are a little deal. Challenge them to fill in the worksheet and then practice having appropriate responses. Tell them you hope they can come back next week and share a time when they started to react to something and then realized it was not really a BIG DEAL and were able to have a little deal reaction. Or, maybe it was a BIG DEAL, but they were able to calmly seek help to fix the problem without yelling, raging, or having a tantrum.

Squad Report

This week our Squad meeting consisted of a discussion around what is a BIG DEAL and what is a little deal. The basic concept is to help children understand that not all problems are BIG problems and how to recognize the difference so they can have correspondingly appropriate reactions. Your child may bring home a copy of their filled in worksheet. We are sending home a blank copy as well so that you can use it to process BIG and little problems that might occur at home or in the community.

It's important to help children have a plan ahead of time to know what issues are BIG and when they are little. Having a specific plan on how to react to those problems may help reduce social isolation due to explosive behavior. We encourage you to use this language throughout the day to share when you see little deals and when you see things that are BIG DEALS. Of course, your modeling of appropriate responses is equally important.

Happy Socializing, from your Squad Leader.

SocialSquad

I forgot my lunch at home today.	I missed my favorite TV show.
I didn't earn all of my rewards or points today.	I lost my homework.
I can't find my pencil.	I can't find my notebook for class.
I broke my pencil.	We have a substitute, and she doesn't say my name correctly.
I'm hungry because my lunch was not food that I like so I didn't eat.	I'm thirsty but forgot to bring a water bottle to class.

Worksheet #21 continued

I only like cheese pizza, and the only pizza offered has pepperoni.	I want to play jump rope, but they are all being used.
I want to play on the big toy at recess, but it is closed because it's too wet.	I only like to play soccer, but the soccer field is closed because they are mowing it.
Students are talking louder than the teacher says we should.	I can't understand the worksheet the teacher just gave me.
My hands hurt when I write too much, and I want to stop, but the teacher says I can't.	I don't like the person I have to sit next to in class.
I can't understand the teacher's instructions.	I have a headache.

SocialSquad

I like using yellow pencils, but the teacher gave me a blue one to use.	Someone asked to borrow my favorite pen.
I smell smoke from a fire inside a building.	I need to use the bathroom right away, but I don't know where to find one.
I hurt my hand at recess, and it starts to bleed.	I see someone fall and hurt their knees. I see blood on their knees, and they are crying.
My mother is very sick, and I'm worried about her, especially if I can't be with her.	My grandpa died recently.
My cat ran away, and I can't find her.	My goldfish is just floating in the tank. I can't tell if it's alive or dead.

Worksheet #21 continued (blank for additional scenarios)

SocialSquad

BIG DEAL or little deal – Worksheet #22

BIG DEAL	Appropriate Response	little deal	Appropriate Response

Lesson 14: Emotion Charades

Lesson 14: Emotion Charades

Materials for this week's group
- A complete set of Emotion Charades Cards (Worksheet #23). These should be printed, cut apart, and laminated for multiple use.

Review
How was the last week? Did you meet the challenge from last week's group? Are there any concerns that anyone has? Next complete a chat session to continue the use of these skills. It may be beneficial to select a chat topic around different emotions. You can have members ask each other, "What makes you happy or what makes you mad?"

Activity/Discussion
Tell members that you are going to play Charades, only it's with a twist. In this game, the object is to identify the emotion that someone is acting out for the rest of the group to guess. Have the adult leaders do a few simple practice emotions, such as sad or happy. Direct the group to take turns guessing and not just shouting out. Encourage them to read all the clues from the actor. Remind them this isn't just facial expression but also body language, which includes head positioning, posture, gestures, etc.

Now have a member choose an Emotion Charade Card. Establish that all actors are to complete their acting without talking or making noises. You may need to give hints to actors on how to show a particular emotion. Make sure that all members have an opportunity to be an actor. Praise all attempts to act as well as to guess the emotions.

For younger or more challenged members, you may need to limit the variety of cards used. For a more advanced play, you could have them guess the emotion as well as who the person (or animal – but they need to specify if it's a person or animal) is that is exhibiting the emotion. For example, Angry Kid or Happy Dog.

This game is a great opportunity to teach members, especially the child of focus, how to "read" other people's emotions.

Mission of the Week
During the next week, find at least two times when you can watch another person and try to figure out what they are feeling. Remember to look at their facial expression as well as their body language. Be prepared to share what you learned when we meet next week.

Squad Report

This week during Social Squad we played Emotion Charades. Members were given turns to silently act out an emotion (which was chosen from a set of cards) for the others to guess. We put a good deal of emphasis on helping members "read" clues from the actors, including facial expressions, head positioning, posture, gestures, etc. Try playing this game at home with your child. Remember to encourage them to look for all the clues.

Happy Socializing, from your Squad Leader.

Emotion Charades Cards – Worksheet #23

Tired	Scared
Happy	Mad
Sad	Anxious
Excited	Focused
Bored	Annoyed
Loving	Confused
Shy	Curious
Guilty	Distracted
Disgusted	Frustrated
Lonely	Embarrassed
Jealous	Surprised
Disappointed	Proud
Sorry	Silly
Brave	Hopeful
Hurt	Insecure

Lesson 15: Mapping Out Choices

Lesson 15: Mapping Out Choices

Materials for this week's group

- Draw Choices Map on white board
- One copy of Choices Map (Worksheet #24) for each member
- One copy of Choices Map Example (Worksheet #25) for adult leader only
- Paper and pens or pencils for all

Review

Have students review how the last week went. Discuss any areas of concern and help problem solve ways to handle that now or in the future.

Discussion

Discuss with members that we all make choices. Sometimes those choices help us get what we want. Sometimes those choices take us on the wrong path, and we end up getting the opposite of what we really wanted. Tell members that today we are going to make a map of how choices lead to outcomes. Give an example of how that can look on a map by showing them the blank map on the white board. Carefully take them through the steps you have on your example worksheet. Share with them that there is always a beginning (box 1) and then the direction is chosen depending on the step that is taken. Tell them each step is indicated by a separate box on the map. Fill in the white board with the example from the worksheet. Take time to discuss the steps. It is best to show the pathway to the positive outcome first and then to show the steps to the undesired outcome.

Once you have shown both pathways, be sure to point out the arrow which indicates that if they recognize they are on the wrong pathway, they can still correct their course and get to the desired outcome. You could share something like, "It's like someone driving a car and taking a wrong turn. If they see the end of the road up ahead is not where they want to be, they can stop, turn around, and get back onto the correct road to take them to where they really wanted to go." This is also a bit like the earlier lesson where members learned to "Flip the Switch."

The importance of this lesson is to teach members, especially the child of focus, that we are all responsible for the choices we make. It is our responsibility to make choices that get us what we want (within reason, of course). This lesson may be difficult for children who have a challenging time understanding how their behaviors impact others. You may need to tie this lesson in with the lesson of Positive and Negative Behavior, reminding students that how we behave has an impact on how others treat us (therefore affecting whether we will get what we want). The main focus will be on personal responsibility and not blaming others for choices we make.

Activity

Now pass out the blank Choices Maps for each student along with pens or pencils. Ask the members to each think of a time when they ended up not getting to something they wanted, and have them fill in the steps in the map on the bottom pathway. Tell them that once they are done, they can think of what different steps might have taken them to what they wanted, and they can fill in those steps on the top pathway. Give them about 10 minutes to fill these in, and then have members share their maps with the group. Use this as a time for peers to give proactive suggestions to the child of focus.

If it will be too challenging for students to fill these in alone, you could do an alternative activity where you all create a scenario together and fill in the blanks together. This will still provide an opportunity for students to understand the concept of a pathway and personal responsibility. Be sure to discuss personal responsibility throughout the activity.

Mission of the Week

Send members home with the filled in Choices Map they have created along with a blank copy they can use at home. Ask them to share the map with an adult and to have the adult help them process a choice during the following week. Encourage members to bring back the maps for a discussion the next week.

Squad Report

This week during Squad, we talked about personal responsibility. We used a Choices Map to help members understand how their actions result in outcomes. We are providing a copy of a blank Choices Map for you to copy and use at home as well as a filled in example to help you see how it works. Your child may also share with you a copy of the map they made today in our meeting. We encourage you to use these maps as a way to process with your child when things do not go as expected for him/her. Be sure to emphasize that it was your child that made the choice to follow a particular path that led to an outcome. You may also choose to use this map in a positive way to show your child how their good choices have led to desired outcomes. This will be helpful in getting them to want to use the map for processing if it isn't always used during negative outcomes.

The map can also be used prior to an activity that you anticipate may be challenging for your child. For example, you might say, "We're going to have dinner at a friend's house tonight, and I'd like us to complete a Choices Map before we go, so you can have a plan that will give you a good outcome." Then, help your child fill in the boxes of the Choices Map which show the two possible outcomes and the steps that could get them there. Remind them they are responsible for their choices and cannot be angry with adults when their choice takes them to the outcome they did not want. Likewise, remind them how happy they will be when they choose the pathway that will lead to the desired outcome. Finally, remind them that they can always switch pathways (via the arrows indicated in the example) if they realize they are headed to the wrong outcome.

Happy Socializing, from your Squad Leader.

SocialSquad

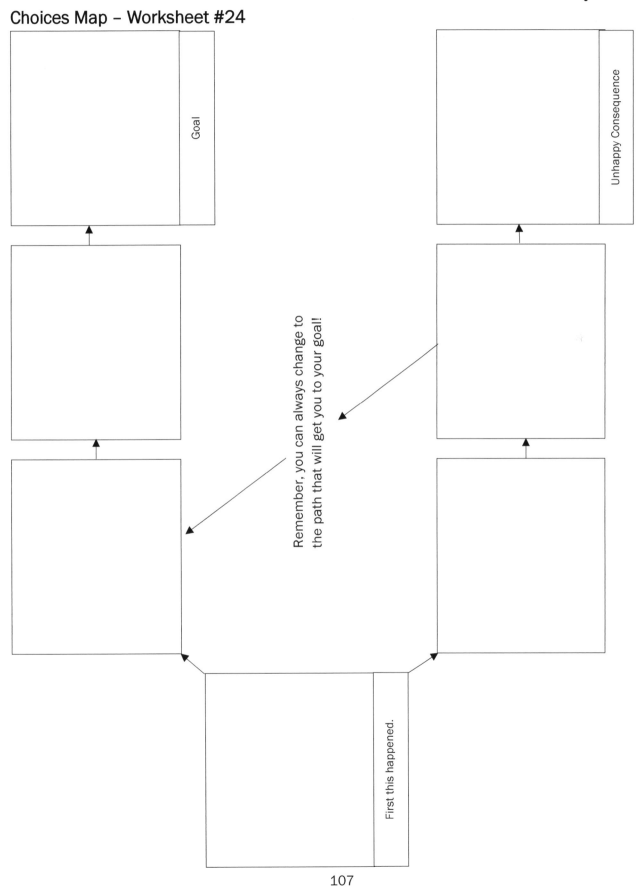

Goal

Unhappy Consequence

Remember, you can always change to the path that will get you to your goal!

First this happened.

Choices Map Example – Worksheet #25

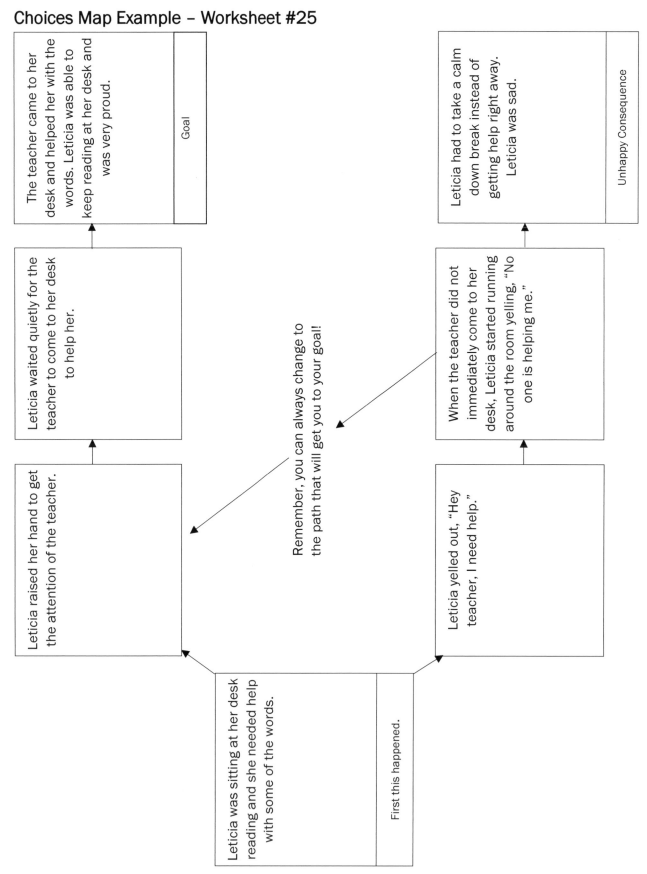

The teacher came to her desk and helped her with the words. Leticia was able to keep reading at her desk and was very proud.

Goal

Leticia had to take a calm down break instead of getting help right away. Leticia was sad.

Unhappy Consequence

Leticia waited quietly for the teacher to come to her desk to help her.

When the teacher did not immediately come to her desk, Leticia started running around the room yelling, "No one is helping me."

Remember, you can always change to the path that will get you to your goal!

Leticia raised her hand to get the attention of the teacher.

Leticia yelled out, "Hey teacher, I need help."

Leticia was sitting at her desk reading and she needed help with some of the words.

First this happened.

108

Lesson 16: The Wrap Up

Lesson 16: The Wrap Up

Materials for this week's group
- Healthy snack for each member
- Napkins
- One copy of Squad Member Final Survey (Worksheet #26) for each member
- Pens or pencils for all

Review/Discussion/Party

Do a quick review of last week's lesson and then share that this is the last formal meeting of the Social Squad. Let members know how much they have been appreciated, and tell them it's time to wrap up the group. Share the snacks and pass out final surveys with instructions to fill in the surveys while enjoying the snacks. After they've had about 10 minutes to fill in the surveys, ask if they'd like to share anything they wrote down. Whether they choose to share or not, be sure to point out a positive change you have seen in each member. Celebrate the successes of the group and the progress made. End the Squad meeting by encouraging all members to continue supporting each other in a positive way.

Be sure to collect the surveys from the children. They should be reviewed to determine if the child of focus and the peers made progress in learning social skills and improving their ability to support one another. As noted in the Squad Report, parents/guardian/teachers are being asked to fill out a final survey (Worksheet #27) as well. This survey should be compared against the beginning survey to determine the effectiveness of the Social Squad. It may be helpful to send a final report to the parents/guardians/teachers to give them your analysis of the progress made by their child. This would be sent after all final surveys have been received.

SocialSquad

Squad Report

Today was our last official Social Squad meeting. We shared a healthy snack and members completed surveys. We celebrated the successes and encouraged all members to continue to support each other in a positive way. As a means for helping us assess the value of this group, we would like for you to fill out a final survey as well. Please complete the attached survey and return it to me. Thank you for entrusting us with the time to help your child grow in the areas of social skills.

May you enjoy many happy social experiences with your child.

Your Squad Leader

Squad Member – Final Survey – Worksheet #26

Member:_____ Date:_____

I enjoyed coming to Social Squad meetings because: _____

_____.

Circle the best answer about you.

More info

1. **People at school play with me.**
   a. always   b. sometimes   c. never _____

2. **I have friends**
   a. always   b. sometimes   c. never _____

3. **I'm happy at school.**
   a. always   b. sometimes   c. never_____

4. **Other children like me.**
   a. always   b. sometimes   c. never _____

5. **I feel safe with children.**
   a. always   b. sometimes   c. never _____

6. **I follow adult directions.**
   a. always   b. sometimes   c. never _____

7. **Changes are ok.**
   a. always   b. sometimes   c. never _____

8. **I do lots of things with other students.**
   a. always   b. sometimes   c. never _____

9. **I like to be alone.**
   a. always   b. sometimes   c. never _____

10. **I want more friends at school.**
    a. always   b. sometimes   c. never _____

SocialSquad

Social Squad Parent/Guardian/Teacher Final Survey – Worksheet #27

Member Name: _____ Date:_____

Filled in by: _____

I continue to have these concerns about my child:_____

_____

I have seen these social skills improve: _____

_____

My child has developed new relationships since participating in a Social Squad:

    ☐YES   ☐NO

Anything else you'd like us to know about your child's experience in a Social Squad:

_____

_____

_____

_____

_____

_____

_____

_____

_____

_____

<u>Page 2 of Parent/Guardian/Teacher Final Survey</u>

Directions: Based on your observations in various situations, rate the child's use of the following skills according to the scale:

1 = child **almost never** uses the skill   4 = child **often** uses the skill
2 = child **seldom** uses the skill   5 = child **almost always** uses the skill
3 = child **sometimes** uses the skill

1) Socially appropriate listening posture _____
   Comment:_____

2) Maintaining a conversation _____
   Comment:_____

3) Starting a conversation _____
   Comment:_____

4) Joining a conversation _____
   Comment:_____

5) Sensitive topics _____
   Comment:_____

6) Playing a game _____
   Comment:_____

7) Asking others to play _____
   Comment:_____

8) Compromising _____
   Comment:_____

9) Keeping calm _____
   Comment:_____

10) Dealing with mistakes _____
    Comment:_____

11) Understanding others' feelings _____
    Comment:_____

12) Dealing with teasing _____
    Comment:_____

13) Maintaining personal space _____
    Comment:_____

Additional Tools & Resources

Additional Tools & Resources

The following pages are tools that may be useful to you in conducting weekly Squad meetings. The top of each page will give a brief description of the purpose of the tool along with instructions for the best use of the tool. Some tools are designed to be used as a proactive support for keeping challenging students involved in the group. Other tools can be used to create your own lessons if you choose to go beyond the 8-10 weeks and feel you need more variety than the lessons that were laid out through Lesson 16.

If you would like even more ideas for continuing the lessons beyond the original scope, we have an Additional Resources List for this as well. The most important concept, as mentioned in the introduction to this manual, is that lessons are best taught with one child of focus and a well-rounded number of positive role models. Again, the idea is for the child of focus to have a group of children with good social skills who are learning social skills alongside them in order to help them generalize more naturally beyond the weekly meetings.

The additional resources recommended include emotion regulation and organizational skills. Often these are both areas of concern for students on the autism spectrum. However, in order not to go too far beyond the realm of lessons directly related to social skills in this manual, we encourage you to use lessons from these other curriculum resources to continue the Social Squad.

Some people have opted to continue Social Squads in a school setting for an entire school year. This is an acceptable approach. However, we encourage you to perhaps change the peer mentors after the first 10+ weeks. You would then have the possibility of repeating some of the lessons for the child of focus without losing the interest of some of the more socially capable members. An added bonus to changing the members of the group is exposing more individuals to the curriculum and having even more support for the child outside of the weekly meetings. Social Squads have also been formed for the same child in consecutive school years so as to increase the level of support.

One added note regarding how to get the most benefit out of Social Squads—sometimes the child of focus is not able to fully understand the lesson(s). However, do not give up hope. We have found that in these cases, it is equally valuable for the peers to recognize this is an area of challenge for the child of focus. It then becomes an opportunity to teach the peers how to compassionately support the student without judgment. This alone has gone a long way to help improve positive relationships for the child of focus as well as to increase their sense of well-being and inclusion.

I Am a Great Participator

The "I Am a Great Participator Motivation Sheet" is intended to be used as a positive reminder/reward chart for children who need extra support in being able to participate in the group. Feel free to adapt the verbiage about what constitutes a good participator based on the unique needs of the child(ren) needing this extra support. Give stickers, smiley faces, or simple check marks ONLY when child is doing the correct behaviors. Do NOT use as a punishment if they are not successful. Children should be reminded with an upbeat voice that they are trying to fill in all of the boxes to show they were a good participator today. Make every effort to keep the interactions positive and give credit for effort even if it is challenging for the group. This motivation sheet can be a powerful reminder for children even without much verbal discussion of its purpose. You can quietly show the child you are giving them credit and continue with the day's lesson without a lot of fanfare, although sometimes you may need to be a little more animated about it to keep them motivated.

I Am a Great Participator Motivation Sheet

I am participating in the group. My body is facing the group and I am looking at the speaker. I am making good comments and waiting my turn to share positive information with my friends.

				I am a great participator!

I am participating in the group. My body is facing the group and I am looking at the speaker. I am making good comments and waiting my turn to share positive information with my friends.

				I am a great participator!

SocialSquad

Icebreaker Tools

The Icebreaker tools can be used as brief starters at the beginning of meetings to help children feel more comfortable and get to know each other better. Any of these could even be substituted for Lesson 2's Activity which is really just a getting-to-know-you activity. There are several different types of icebreakers listed here, and you should only use one per week. Some of these icebreakers will take up quite a bit of the weekly meeting, so they should either be modified or used as a sort of substitute lesson for that week. Some would work well for a group that has been running for a while and could be used as an additional lesson on how to get to know people better.

Icebreakers are used to warm up the group and encourage interaction as a team. It's also a great way for group members to learn more about each other. In the beginning they may not know much about each other, but through these fun activities they will have a better understanding of the other members' interests.

It may be helpful to have a note taker keep track of people's responses and use these as a source of information for the child of focus to have a visual reminder about their friends' interests. When you have students in a group who have autism or issues with thinking outside the box, they may struggle over answering open-ended questions. If this is the case, reframe the questions so that answers can be yes/no or multiple choice. Given enough experience, members will eventually get better at answering these types of questions.

Quick Starter Questions

The following questions or sentence starters can be used as icebreakers. It is recommended to use one and only one at each team meeting.

1. What is your favorite movie/book/video game?
2. If you could be an animal, what would it be and why?
3. Do you have a pet? If yes, what type of animal is it and what's its name?
4. Who is the most important person in your life?
5. What I want to learn about from my friends in this group is………
6. What would you do if someone gave you $1,000?
7. What is your favorite season of the year and why?
8. What is the hardest thing you've ever had to do?
9. What is the thing you worry about the most?
10. What is the strangest food you've ever had to eat?
11. Think back to when you were very little. What's your first memory?
12. What do you think you will be doing in five years?
13. One of the things people like the most about me is………….
14. Name the one thing you like most about yourself.
15. What do you think would be a perfect age to be and why?
16. If you could go anywhere in the world, where would it be?
17. What is the best gift someone ever gave you? Why was it the best?
18. Were you named after someone special or does your name mean something special?
19. Who is your favorite cartoon or anime character?
20. When you look back over the last week, what is the best thing that happened to you?

Here are some questions or sentence starters that can be used once the group has been meeting for several weeks. These will help members to share at a deeper level. They will also help teach the child of focus how to learn more about friends he/she may already have.

1. What is one thing you don't like about being a part of this group?
2. What is one thing you like best about being a part of this group?
3. I think the person in this group who enjoys life the most is........
4. Now that we've been meeting for a while, who have you learned the most about in this group?
5. What person in this group would you like to learn more about?
6. What is something you would like this group to know about you that you've been a little afraid to talk about before?
7. What is something you'd like to have change about the group meetings?
8. Name one thing you've done outside of the group meetings with each individual person in the last few weeks.
9. If there was one thing you could change about yourself, what would it be?
10. What is your most challenging social situation? (e.g., eating corn on the cob in front of friends, calling someone on the phone that you've never called before, finding someone to sit with at lunchtime.)

Fact or Fiction?

Give each member a pencil and paper. Have them write down two true things about themselves and one thing about themselves that is not true. Take turns having the members each read their three "facts." Coach them not to give away truth or fiction by their facial expressions, tone of voice, or body language. Encourage members to listen quietly until all facts are read for an individual before making guesses as to which one is the false fact.

It's Your Choice

Put a line of tape down the middle of an open space long enough for all the members to stand on at one time. Have members straddle the tape. You will ask, "Would you rather … ," and then fill in with the questions below. Members will jump to the right or left of the line depending on which side you indicate for each choice.

The questions below are just some ideas, but feel free to expand the questions based on what you know about the group already. Some questions are silly so encourage members to have fun and not to take it too seriously even if the choices are serious.

Do this activity for about 10 minutes and then have members sit down and discuss how it's sometimes easy and yet sometimes hard to make choices. Sometimes we don't like either choice, but we still have to choose. Remind them it may be like that at school or in social situations. Have peers discuss how they handle their feelings about these situations.

- Lose your ability to walk or to talk?
- Own a frog or a snake?
- Spend a vacation at the beach or in the mountains?
- Always be cold or always be hot?
- Be completely bald or have hair all over your body?
- Jump from an airplane or a boat?
- Never eat your favorite food or never see your favorite TV show again?
- Be famous for saving someone's life or for inventing something popular?
- Eat spinach or cauliflower?
- Be completely alone on a desert island or be stranded there with someone you don't like?
- Wrestle an alligator or a tiger?
- Be taller or shorter than you are right now?

What if.....

All of the questions below need to be written on 3x5 index cards and placed face down in the middle of the table. Determine who should start and then instruct them to pick the top card. They will then turn to the person next to them, address them by name, and read the question on the card. The student then needs to respond with an answer or comment about the statement. That card needs to be placed at the bottom of the pile, and then the activity is repeated around the table.

This is not only a good activity for helping the members learn more about each other, but it also promotes good social skills. The skills worked on are directing questions at a person, waiting for a response, and then ending the discussion.

- If you had a chance to learn a new skill, what would it be?
- If you could go live in space for a year, what three things would you take with you?
- If you had to have an allergy, what would you want to be allergic to?
- If you had one day to live over, what day would you pick?
- If you could only wear clothes that were all one color, what color would you choose?
- If you could change one thing about yourself, what would it be?
- If your mom said "I'm cooking your favorite meal," what would it be?
- If you lived on a farm, what pet would you want to have?
- If you could ask the governor of our state one question, what would you ask?
- If we had a TV in the room right now, what would you want to watch?
- If you found out you were the only boy or the only girl invited to a party, what would you do?
- If you could visit any place in the world, where would it be?
- If you found $100 in the street, what would you do with the money?
- If you could study any animal, what would it be?
- If you were able to skip one class every day, what would it be?
- If you had money to buy a car, what car would you choose?
- If your family had to move to another state, what state would you want it to be?
- If you won $1,000, how would you spend the money?
- If you could eat as much of one flavor of ice cream as you wanted, what flavor would you choose?
- If you could skip a day of the week, what day would you skip?

Belief Masks

Materials: 8x10 white card stock paper (one for each member); pencils; crayons, markers or paint; and scissors.

Have each member (don't forget to include the adults) draw and cut out a life-size face shape from the white paper, including eyes and mouth. Tell members to decorate the left side of the face with things that represent what the person believes other people see, know, or believe about them from the outside. The right side of the face should be decorated to represent what the person feels about themselves and things that are going on inside (things others may not see or know about).

This activity should be done after several weeks together so that members will feel comfortable talking about themselves more openly. Once the art portion is done, have each member share their mask with the rest of the group. Be prepared to discuss self-image and self-worth.

More importantly, with individuals with ASD, be prepared to help them understand that different people have different perspectives and that others do not always see things in the same way. Don't be surprised if these individuals use the same representations on both sides of their mask, because they truly believe that others see them as they see themselves. This is a great opportunity to teach them valuable lessons about perspective taking and the need to share internal information and not assume others know what they're thinking.

Friend Fact Bingo

This game is designed to help the child of focus learn appropriate ways to ask other people questions and to encourage them to ask a variety of people, not focus on just one person.

Ahead of time: Make a 5 x 4 grid and fill in each box with one of the statements below. Feel free to create your own statements that are applicable to your particular group. Print enough copies of the "bingo card" for each member to have one.

During the group meeting, give each member a preprinted card and pens or pencils. The goal is for each member to talk to all of the other members at least one time each and ask them if any of the statements on their bingo cards are true about them. If an item listed on the card relates to the person they are talking with, they have the person initial that box on their card.

Allow about 10 minutes for the activity and then have each member share at least one interesting fact they discovered about another group member.

- Has blue eyes
- Loves Justin Bieber
- Has a sister
- Owns a bike
- Loves the color blue
- Walks to school
- Knows what a quark is (it's a tiny theoretical particle that makes up protons and neutrons in the atomic nucleus)
- Has ridden on a train
- Is wearing red
- Has visited another country
- Loves to ride horses
- Has played at least two different video games this week
- Has a name beginning with 'T'
- Loves Mexican food
- Plays a musical instrument
- Hates spinach
- Knows the capital of every state in the USA
- Plays soccer
- Likes to get up early, even on the weekend
- Wants to study quantum physics
- Loves the TV show Survivor
- Has more than one pet
- Knows what job they want as a grown person

Positive Thoughts/Negative Thoughts Game

The Positive Thoughts/Negative Thoughts Game is a tool that was designed to practice the skills learned in Lesson 10: Positive or Negative Behaviors.

Cut out the two statements and glue or tape them to two separate boxes or containers with open lids or slots cut in the top. Next, copy and cut the scenarios into individual cards. Note that there are blanks for you to fill in with scenarios that you feel need to be addressed for your specific Squad members, especially the child of focus. (Social Squad logo cards are also included. You can use them for the backs of the scenario cards to make a sturdy deck to use over and over if you'd like. Copy and cut out the backs, adhere to the scenario pieces, and laminate.)

Turn all the scenario pieces face down, and have members take turns choosing one at a time. When they choose a scenario, they read it aloud and then state whether that behavior would make a person have positive or negative thoughts about them. Then the group decides if they are accurate. This may take some extra prompting from adults to make correct choices and to discuss why it is a correct choice. Have members place it in the correct container, and continue play with others taking their turns in the same way.

THINGS THAT MIGHT MAKE PEOPLE HAVE NEGATIVE THOUGHTS ABOUT ME!

THINGS THAT WILL PROBABLY MAKE PEOPLE HAVE POSITIVE THOUGHTS ABOUT ME.

I am in middle school, and I like to play with small toys. I bring them out and play with them during lessons or act things out with them on top of my desk.	When I join a group of people that are having a conversation, I usually listen quietly for a few minutes so that I can find out what they're talking about before I make any comments.
I sometimes get excited to answer a question or make a comment during class, and I blurt out instead of raising my hand. I do this at least four times a day.	When someone I don't like to spend time with asks me to come hang out, I usually say "Oh man, I really can't today but maybe some other time."
I see a lot of people acting silly at different times, but I'm not really sure why people think it's funny or when it's okay to do those things. So I just act silly whenever I want and say goofy things without looking to see other people's reactions.	When someone I don't feel comfortable around asks to sit next to me at lunch, I just tell them honestly how I feel. I say something like, "Sorry, but you're chewing noises are too gross for me to eat around."
Whenever I want to join a group at a lunchroom table, I just sit down in the middle of the group with my lunch and start talking.	I love getting reactions for making body noises. I'm really good at pretending to burp or pass gas.

When someone starts talking about a topic that bothers me, I can't help myself. I just start crying and telling them they have to stop.	Sometimes I start talking about things that I'm interested in and forget to let other people take a turn to talk. I even forget to ask them about their interests.
I can't help myself when I hear someone making body noises. I just bust out laughing at them, even in the middle of class.	My skin is really sensitive, and sometimes it itches or feels weird. It helps if I scratch it a lot or pick at it for a while.
People say that teenagers should start wearing deodorant, but I kind of like the smell of sweat, so I won't bother using deodorant.	I hate feeling left out of games or picked on in the middle of a game. I think if I whine about it, maybe people will understand and be nice to me.
I always put on deodorant when I'm getting ready for school in the morning and again when I finish with P.E.	People fascinate me, and I love to watch them. Sometimes I can stare at the same person for at least five minutes.

SocialSquad

I have short hair so I don't feel like I really need to comb it every day. That's a good thing because I don't like to bother with things like hygiene.

I can't stand to miss phone calls or text messages. I check my phone a lot wherever I am, even in class or during a movie.

When I'm in a class or in a group of kids, I use whole body listening.

I love to make shapes with the food on my plate. I even like to roll it in my hands and pull it apart.

I like to ask other students what they've been doing. I usually say something like, "What did you do last night?" or "Are you doing anything fun this weekend?"

I hear some kids calling other kids mean or weird names. Some kids laugh about this, but I never call names or laugh because I think it is mean.

When I'm really interested in an activity, I hate to stop and then start something new. So I usually just ignore the teacher's directions and keep on doing what I was doing until I'm finished.

Sometimes other people talk about things I'm not really interested in. But if I listen and respond to them about their interests, we will eventually get to talk about what interests me.

Sometimes I get my feelings hurt, and I'm not sure how to react. I usually try to take a few breaths and think about whether someone really meant what they said. I try to think about their perspective instead of exploding.	People sometimes ask me to stop doing things, like repeating a joke or asking someone for the same thing over and over again. I'm confused about this because I really like doing it, and the other people should just get used to me. So I usually ignore them and keep doing what I'm doing.
I saw someone drop a book on the floor, so I picked it up and handed it to them.	I like to share my candy or popcorn treats that I get at lunchtime.
I noticed that my best friend had their pants zipper undone. I quietly whispered to them that they should fix the problem.	When I'm having a conversation with other kids, it's sometimes hard to stay on topic. But I do my best to stay on the same topic.
When a girl I know had a piece of food stuck between her teeth, I laughed and said, "Are you saving that food for a snack?" I said this in front of a lot of other people.	When I see kids laughing at another kid, I just walk up and push them away to protect the kid who is being laughed at, and then I tell the kid he's stupid for letting them bully him.

Brushing my teeth makes them feel great and makes me want to smile a lot.	I'm pretty shy, but I'm making an effort to say "hi" to at least one new person every day.

Additional Resource List

Books

These books provide great material for additional lessons to teach beyond those scripted out in this manual. We recommend using the first four lessons directly from the Social Squad manual before trying to incorporate these other materials. The additional lessons found in these books can be used in between lessons 5 through 15 or can be tacked on at the end.

Hygiene and Related Behaviors for Children and Adolescents with Autism Spectrum and Related Disorders: A Fun Curriculum with a Focus on Social Understanding by Kelly J. Mahler, MS, OTR/L.

Teaching Children EMPATHY, The Social Emotion: Lessons, Activities and Reproducible Worksheets (K-6) That Teach How to "Step Into Others' Shoes" by Tonia Caselman, Ph.D.

Diary of a Social Detective: Real-Life Tales of Mystery, Intrigue and Interpersonal Adventure by Jeffrey E. Jessum, Ph.D.

The Zones of Regulation by Leah M. Kuypers, MA Ed, OTR/L

The MindUP Curriculum by the Hawn Foundation

Superflex ... A Superhero Social Thinking Curriculum by Stephanie Madrigal and Michelle Garcia Winner
*You can use this curriculum in place of the lessons for kindergarten-aged children. The key is to teach these lessons in a group with their typical peers.

Games

These games can be used to practice lessons learned throughout the course of the Social Squad meetings.

Whoonu by Cranium

Should I? or Shouldn't I? What Would Others Think?™ by Dominique Baudry, MS., Ed, Social Thinking Publishing.

Apples to Apples® by Mattel

Hedbanz by Spin Master Games

You Gotta Be Kidding! by Zobmondo!!

SocialSquad

About the Authors

Nicole Bain, PhD, is a licensed Psychologist in the state of Washington. She completed her pre-doctorate internship at Seattle Children's Hospital and the University of Washington Center on Human Development and Disability (CHDD) with an emphasis on neurodevelopmental assessments. In addition, Dr. Bain completed a two year post-doctorate at the University of Washington at the Center on Human Development and Disabilities through the Leadership Education in Neurodevelopmental Disabilities (LEND) program focusing on neurodevelopmental assessments and Autism Spectrum Disorder (ASD). She earned a Masters in Counseling Psychology from Pepperdine University and Masters in School Psychology from the University of Washington.

Dr. Bain has been in private practice for the past five years working with families and children with disabilities. The majority of her clientele have ASD. In addition, she conducts trainings in the community, at universities, and in the schools for parents and professionals on interventions for individuals on the Autism Spectrum. Recently, she has joined a non-profit organization (the Wa-Gro foundations). Through this organization, Dr. Bain has provided training on autism to medical practitioners, psychologists, and special education teachers in Zihuatanejo, Mexico. Dr. Bain also worked as the Autism Instructional Coordinator for the Edmonds School District for five years. In this role, she creates programs for students on the Autism Spectrum and educates school staff and peers about autism, related behaviors, and ways to provide support to students on the spectrum. Dr. Bain has published two articles in research journals during her professional career.

Dr. Bain was inspired to obtain the above credentials due to a true passion for working with children, which came 12 years ago when she was an in-home ABA therapist for a young girl with autism. The girl was able to make many amazing gains through the therapy both academically and behaviorally, but there was one large piece of the puzzle still missing; she wanted to make a friend, someone who truly understood her and wanted to play with her. From that point on Dr. Bain made it her focus of therapy to find children in the neighborhood who were making attempts to initiate play with the young girl but were unsure how to do this successfully. Through educating the peers about the little girl's behaviors and how to engage her, friendships were formed. Years later, the girl's mother reported that these friendships remained throughout her school years. From this rewarding and life-changing experience, Dr. Bain was committed to creating a curriculum and so the idea of Social Squad was formed.

Kathie Davis is the parent of a 32-year-old daughter with multiple disabilities. Ms. Davis has educated herself about the many aspects involved in her daughter's disabilities through books, seminars, and college courses. While she does not hold a degree, her extensive knowledge as a parent was valuable in the development of this social skills curriculum.

In addition to her parenting expertise, Ms. Davis worked as a paraprofessional in special education preschool and elementary school programs in the Edmonds School District for approximately ten years. She has been a member of the District's Autism Team as an Autism Support Specialist for the last ten years. In this role, she has been a consultant to general education as well as special education teachers, school counselors, psychologists, behavior specialists, and speech and language pathologists. In the last eight years, she has continued to hone her skills through attending as well as presenting at numerous workshops within the district and community.

As part of her role as Autism Support Specialist for the school district, Ms. Davis has helped form and lead multiple small groups for children with social challenges to learn social skills alongside peer mentors. She has also lead social skills groups in private practice with Dr. Bain.

Ms. Davis is a confident speaker in the local disability community. She has many connections with community programs for people with disabilities, including the ARC of Snohomish County, Special Olympics and Banchero Disability Partners. It has become her mission to help educate others about disabilities and to help foster inclusion of persons with disabilities and their families.

socialsquads@gmail.com

Made in the USA
Middletown, DE
21 January 2017